MAKING THE LAW WORK FOR YOU: A GUIDE FOR SMALL BUSINESSES

MAKING THE LAW WORK FOR YOU: A GUIDE FOR SMALL BUSINESSES

JEROME S. RICE & KEITH LIBBEY

Contemporary Books, Inc.
chicago

Library of Congress Cataloging in Publication Data

Rice, Jerome S.
  Making the law work for you.

  Includes index.
  1. Small business—Law and legislation—
United States. I. Libbey, Keith, 1937–
joint author. II. Title.
KF1659.R5   346.73′0652   79-8748
ISBN 0-8092-7111-7
ISBN 0-8092-7110-9 pbk.

Published by Contemporary Books, Inc.
180 North Michigan Avenue, Chicago, Illinois 60601
Manufactured in the United States of America
Library of Congress Catalog Card Number: 79-8748
International Standard Book Number: 0-8092-7111-7 (cloth)
                                    0-8092-7110-9 (paper)

Published simultaneously in Canada by
Beaverbooks
953 Dillingham Road
Pickering, Ontario L1W 1Z7
Canada

Contents

Introduction

As today's business world becomes increasingly complex, a legislative explosion is adding entire bodies of law to the already swollen statute books. Regulatory agencies continue to promulgate regulations at the local, state, and national levels. Environmentalists, organized labor, minorities, and job safety advocates are all armed with legal weapons as never before. As business itself grows more complex in an increasingly anonymous society, litigiousness is on the increase. It is much easier to sue a stranger than a neighbor. What does all this mean to the beleaguered businessman?* In the eyes of the authors of this book, it means that today's businessman cannot afford to ignore legal considerations when he makes traditional business decisions. Just as preventive maintenance can eliminate unnecessary equipment breakdowns, advance legal preparation can avert legal disasters. The aim of this book, therefore, is to help the businessman who has no legal training become legally prepared. If he uses it properly, he will find that the law can serve his business, rather than suffocate it. As authors (one, a specialist in organizing, planning, and financing businesses; and the other, a litigator experienced in working out conflict situations for business-men), we believe we can help educate you beneficially by focusing on specific problems as seen from our perspectives. We feel the most intelligent method of doing this is to take the most common legal business-problems we have encountered during our collective thirty-four years of legal experience and inform you of the considerations that we deem most impor-tant in dealing with them. We attempt to "step into the shoes" of the businessman. This seems a much more practical ap-proach than attempting a survey of the entire field of legal considerations involved in a business. Such a survey would be much too unwieldy for the layman. Consequently, this book is a distillation of conclusions drawn from our years of experience in applying legal theories to particular cases. We do not burden the reader with the great amount of legal theory behind our conclusions. And wherever possible, we have avoided legal jargon. Hopefully, by pointing out some of the legal rocks, reefs, and shoals encountered by businessmen, we will help you pilot your business toward greater success.

---

*Throughout this book your authors have used the masculine pronoun *businessman* out of habit and because of the unwieldiness of the term *busi-nessperson*. No offense is meant to any of the fine businesswomen we have known and whom we hope find this book useful; and, if any is taken, we respectfully apologize.

MAKING THE LAW WORK FOR YOU: A GUIDE FOR SMALL BUSINESSES

1

Leverage on Your Lender

Troubled businesses are likely to have trouble with their lenders. Trouble can take many forms, ranging from polite questions and concern about the adequacy of *collateral* to collection actions. Typically, there are plenty of warnings before the storm actually hits. It is important to start your preparations to weather the storm at the warning stage.

Every businessman's objective in dealing with his lenders should be to keep him happy and quiet. A nervous banker is trouble whether or not there is a real problem with the loan. There are so many opportunities for a lender to make a judgment call on a loan, even when its objective *quality* is not in question, that you can rarely rely solely on quality to help you secure advantageous terms—unless, of course, your name is IBM. Even if the lender's nervousness does not result in a *default* notice, he may restrict credit, refuse to renew the loan, regard some collateral as unacceptable, raise the interest rate, require an expensive field warehousing arrangement, or take

1

some other harmful action. Therefore, it's always best to keep your lender happy. If he wants financial statements more often, supply them. If he wants you to file some new documents without adding new collateral, do it. Don't insist on your contractual rights in unimportant matters. If there is no contract, don't refuse requests on the grounds that they're a waste of time or constitute "paper shuffling." Keep your lender informed; send him information. If you're making a change in the business, even if it doesn't require consent, supply him with information about it.

If everything fails and your lender becomes nervous or calls a default, then matters change. You are not defenseless. A vigorous contest or negotiation does, in some cases, produce a satisfactory conclusion, even in the midst of a financial disaster.

Delay is the principal weapon available to the borrower. The lender knows this and will often make concessions to avoid delay. Another weapon is the right to attack the way the lender has handled the loan or *foreclosure* process, or the validity of his documents.

In recent years, a number of cases and laws have severely restricted foreclosure procedures. Failure of the lender to observe these restrictions adds an arrow to the borrower's quiver. And quite often, inexperienced lenders fail to achieve proper documentation of loans. Attacking a lender for these failures resembles the approach of the experienced criminal lawyer who, when confronted with overwhelming evidence of a guilty client, will put the prosecutor on trial—or the star witness, or the police—in hopes that the jury will lose sight of the defendant amidst all the smoke.

Lenders have been successfully attacked for agreeing to a large line of credit and then restricting the credit available. If the borrower relies on such an assurance and expands his business so that more working capital is needed, only to find it cut off by the lender, he can make a claim against the lender and immediately seek an injunction against any foreclosure action.

The major delay threat is that of *bankruptcy*. *Secured*

lenders, in particular, want no part of bankruptcy. While their collateral position is legally protected in a proceeding, they may have to wait six months to a year for permission from the court to *liquidate collateral.* Meanwhile the value of the collateral is substantially reduced. One can get significant concessions with the veiled threat of bankruptcy. It can be helpful to state that "schedules" are being prepared and a petition drafted so that a filing can be done quickly. Be sure to have a few thousand dollars available to get this work done and to pay the filing fees. A bankruptcy lawyer will want an advance payment. These fees are subject to the bankruptcy court's scrutiny as to fairness but are generally not vulnerable to being set aside. The news that one has hired a bankruptcy expert will have a sobering effect on the lender.

Other steps should be taken at an early stage. Make sure you have copies of all the documents in effect between you and the lender. Scrutinize these with your own lawyer for legal defects. Has the lender failed to file in the right office? Has he described the collateral erroneously? Has he got your name wrong? Have you moved your offices to another county or state without new filings? Is the note *usurious*? Any one of these defects can leave the lender unsecured and vulnerable. He may not have the *leverage* he thought he had; so he may agree to additional time, or even extend more credit.

Additional time allows you to arrange *refinancing.* This alternative should be explored early, so there is time to allow a new lender to analyze your credit situation. Finance companies are often a source of funds when banks get cold feet. They are more accustomed to managing problem loans. Unfortunately, their rates reflect this. You should expect a tighter loan agreement and strict collateral management procedures. Stay away from finance companies whose loan officers want a personal gratuity before they will recommend a loan.

Sometimes it is possible, in this early period, to reduce your *exposure.* Payments can be directed first to lenders holding personal guarantees. These payments will not be *preferences* (which the trustee in bankruptcy may set aside) if the party paid off has *priority* over other creditors, or if the payments are made more than three months prior to bankruptcy. Remember, personal guarantees are not extinguished by the bankruptcy of the company, but only by the bankruptcy of the *guarantor*. Similar items to consider are the payment of FICA payroll taxes. Personal liability to the government for these unpaid taxes falls on the officers and directors who control the disposition of funds for the company. The law purports to place personal liability on *all* officers and directors, but actual cases have been more restrictive in assigning liability. Incidentally, if you're an outside officer or director of a corporation in trouble, resign early, or make sure payroll taxes are currently being paid.

Once you discover a weakness in the lender's position, determine the best time to announce it. Don't wait until you're in court. Meet with lender and his counsel. Demonstrate the weakness in his position. Offer a reasonable proposal that shows how he may improve his position by going along with you. Suggest the calamity that will befall him if the situation collapses and all creditors descend simultaneously on your company. At this stage, candor and forthrightness are important. You're asking the lender to have more faith in you and your plan. Recognize the risks he is taking, and your own weaknesses, and state how you'll deal with them. Don't brush them aside. The borrower who is blind to his peril will never persuade lenders to go along one more time. This is another point at which your efforts in the past to keep your lender happy and relaxed will pay off. The lender has to make a judgment based on few objective standards. Frequently, this judgment will turn on his feeling of "confidence" in management. This is a personal matter strongly influenced by past relations.

In conclusion, let us offer this word of encouragement. It has always astounded us how often lenders are susceptible to attack at one or more of the points mentioned above. Receipt of a "pay or die" letter from your lender does not necessarily require you to do either one.

2

Negotiating Loans

Learn as much as you can from your lawyer or from a number of bankers before you ask for a loan. When the lender is still trying to "sell" you his money, he will make concessions not available later on in the deal.

Check around with other businessmen to find out what rates are current and what kinds of deals they have made. If you are not locked in with one lender, check with two or three others. At any given time, different lenders will offer different terms, depending on the cost of money that each is encountering. In 1979, for example, one major finance company met its profit goals for the year in the first half. Then it decided to go for a bigger *market share*. The firm cut its rate to 3 percent over *prime,* with no requirement for a compensating balance (which is the practice of requiring the borrower to leave 10 percent or so of the loan on deposit with the lender), compared to the competition's rate of 5 percent to 7 percent over prime. Some banks have peak deposits in the fall and need to

5

put the money to work. All of this can yield a cost advantage to the sophisticated borrower.

Some of the items to put on your negotiating list are the following; at least discuss them early so you know where you stand.

1. **Bank's lawyer's fees** Ask the bank to absorb them. They often do. If not, negotiate a maximum figure that you will pay.

2. **Loan fees or minimum charges** Finance companies are more likely to charge these fees. The banks are better able to pick up the extra income they want through account relationships, such as checking accounts, safe deposits, and trust services (which may not be an extra cost for you at all—you must bank somewhere). Refinancing penalties (the charge for early repayment of a term loan) can be a real problem if rates drop in the future and you wish to reduce your interest costs.

3. **Compensating balances** Banks will often require the borrower to leave 5 percent or 10 percent of the loan balance on deposit in the borrower's account. This has the effect of increasing the effective interest rate by 1 percent or 2 percent and also reduces the amount available on the *line of credit.* Include this factor in your calculation of the comparative borrowing costs.

4. **Insurance** Lenders sometimes require insurance on a loan, or strongly suggest it. There is nothing wrong with this, but it is illegal for them to require you to buy from them or an affiliated insurance agency.

5. **Covenants** Affirmative covenants (things you must do during the term of the loan) and negative covenants (things you must not do during the term of the loan) can range from harmless (e.g., maintain your corporate existence and supply annual financial statements), to a straight jacket (e.g., no additional debt, tight current and long term ratios, no increases in officers' compensation, and the like). Find out what the bank has in mind, and get rid of the covenants most

objectionable to your particular business. Your best argument is that you cannot live with the proposed covenant for reasons peculiar to your business. Be prepared to state specific reasons or give concrete examples. Lenders generally listen to such arguments. The purpose of the covenants is to set parameters of performance rather than to allow daily control of the business by the banker.

6. **Default provisions** Businessmen often overlook these as *boiler plate.* They can be crucial. Always get a grace period of ten to thirty days added to the default provisions, within which you can cure the default. This will prevent trouble in case of inadvertent failure to make an interest payment on time or late delivery of a financial report. Couple the grace period with a requirement that written notice of default be received before the grace period begins. Frequently, lenders will allow several additional days to go by before a written notice goes out. You'd be surprised how much refinancing or how many other arrangements you can accomplish in a few days when you're up against a serious default. In that case, you'd better have negotiated the extra time in advance.

7. **Representations and warranties** Don't agree to anything that isn't true or that you cannot be sure about. Requirements that you *represent* that you have "adequate" capital for your business or that your company is not subject to any requirements more onerous than those of your competition are not acceptable because you cannot know what your competition is subject to. As a compromise on these kinds of issues you may say that *to the best of your knowledge* they are true; otherwise, you risk being in default as soon as you sign the agreement. Be wary of the requirement that the agreements being signed are enforceable in accordance with their terms. You should couple this with an exception for equitable remedies in general. Otherwise, you are representing that the agreement is specifically enforceable against you, which may be a *far more difficult matter.* The remedy of specific enforcement is an equitable remedy requiring you to actually perform the act in

question. This differs from the normal remedy at law which is damages.

8. **Term and termination of the agreement** How long is the lender bound to keep his loan outstanding to you? Is this to be a *term loan* or *demand loan*? If it is a demand loan and you have a seasonal business, be sure that the agreement contains some restrictions on when the lender can act, or requires lengthy notice, such as three to six months, before he can cut off your credit. Particularly in inventory and accounts receivable financing situations that involve a lock-box delivery system (whereby all of your checks go to the lender and he then readvances funds to you against the available collateral) your life's blood is in his control. If he decides to terminate the loan, he may collect all of your receivables and advance nothing back to you until he has been paid off. This can be devastating. You should provide yourself with some protection by refusing him the right to terminate advances. The other aspect of the advance formula is the finance company's typical request that it have the right to reduce the formula for advances at any time, without notice. Some restrictions should be placed upon this right, including a time period in which you can refinance so long as you are not in default.

9. **Direct payment** Lenders frequently request the right to notify accounts receivable debtors to pay them directly. This should be limited by the restriction that they can only do so after default.

10. **Right to a hearing** Loans sometimes include a provision that you waive your right to a hearing in court in the event of default and foreclosure. This eliminates one of your major weapons in the event of a misunderstanding or a default of some kind under the agreement. The right to a hearing will provide you with delay and may expose the lender to legal attack in the hearing that he won't want to risk.

Lenders will sometimes back down from all of the above positions, given enough negotiating effort on your part.

3

Signing Notes

A signature on a note can create several quite different liabilities. A signer can be a *co-maker,* a guarantor, a *surety,* an *endorser,* or a *primary* or *secondary party.* Care should be taken to get it right at the time of signing. Your ultimate liability will turn on the form of the signature and the understanding then created.

Signatures at the foot of the note, which on their face refer back to the words "The undersigned hereby promises to pay . . ."—or similar words—are the signatures of co-makers or primary parties. The signers are jointly and severally liable for the full amount due, which means that each of them can be made to pay the full amount, but each also has a claim for contribution from the others.

At the opposite extreme is a signature on the back of the note after the legend "Collection of this note is guaranteed by X." This creates a secondary party liability that is enforceable only after the primary party has been pursued and found unable to pay. The secondary party has a right to ultimately collect in full from the primary party. A co-maker, on the other hand, collects only a proportionate share of the balance from his co-makers (unless there is an agreement to the contrary), not the full amount; although he may have been required to pay it all himself.

The secondary party under a *guarantee of collection* has certain defenses available to him. Failure of consideration, improper release of the primary obligor, extension of time, and failure to give notice are defenses provided by law.

An example of the operation of one of these defenses is the case where there are two or more co-makers of a note. The note is renewed without the signature of one of the co-makers. Is he liable later on, upon default under the note? If the original note contained consent language to renewals or extensions of the indebtedness, the nonsigner is generally liable. On the other hand if the new note is intended by the parties to substitute for the old note, or to satisfy the old debt with a new one, then the nonsigner is generally held to be released. It is generally held that the burden of showing an intention to satisfy the old note is on the nonsigner. This could be done by showing that the lender acquiesced in the new note without the co-signer knowing that the two parties had terminated their business relationship, and by showing that the signer had indicated responsibility for the business and the debt.

If, rather than being a co-maker, the secondary party on the note is only a surety (e.g. he did not receive any of the consideration, but signed only as an accommodation maker), he has an additional defense. He may well escape liability by showing that the lender renewed the note without any express reservation of rights against him. An express reservation of rights could take the form of a letter to the nonsigner so stating.

Another issue that arises in the context of guarantees is whether a corporation can guarantee a debt of its shareholder, officer, or its parent corporation. Conversely, if it has been done, is it enforceable against the corporation?

Some states have laws prohibiting this type of transaction. More modern laws permit such transactions. Actual cases reveal a tendency by the courts to enforce such guarantees. Nonetheless, there are cases to the contrary. Careful bank lawyers will try to avoid setting up such a transaction and will not always feel they are on solid ground in trying to collect on the guarantee. One of the fundamental questions is whether the corporation received a direct benefit from the guarantee or whether the guarantee was made solely for the benefit of the shareholder, officer, or parent corporation. The reason for the rule is to protect other creditors of the corporation making the guarantee from diversion of corporate assets to the benefit of other persons. Consequently, care should be exercised in setting up such a transaction in the first place, likewise, one might look for this form of defense in case of liability.

4

Collecting Slow and Bad Accounts

CLASSIFICATION

Collections may require differences in approach from business to business. What may simply be "slow pay" to some businesses is an alarming, probable bad debt to others. For example, it is not uncommon for the collections of law firms to run months behind because of the amount of time necessary to complete matters. On the other hand, in some retail businesses, any account over thirty days old is automatically turned over to collection. The authors strongly recommend an intelligent classification of accounts in order to distinguish between slow pay and bad debts. This probably requires some organized process of receivables aging. If your bookkeeping system does not allow this, it is probably obsolete. Once again, however, there may be certain industry-wide characteristics which dictate flexibility, such as the seasons with regard to agricultural accounts.

Once a receivables aging procedure has been tailored for

your business—taking into account the industry-wide characteristics of your business, its seasons, and other considerations—which you have perhaps fine-tuned to take into account the individual characteristics of your accounts, you can more intelligently look for signs which spell a bad debt requiring immediate action. A few such signs of trouble are the following:

1. Disputes that involve a sudden change of posture by an account. For example challenging the quality of the goods, timeliness of delivery, wording of contracts, etc., are definite danger signals, perhaps indicating that the account is attempting to buy time while he juggles his debts.

2. Checks returned due to insufficient funds (NSF checks).

3. Dramatic changes in dealing with you, without logical explanation, such as sudden failure to pay on a certain date of the month, sudden change of bank on a check, payment by money order rather than check, payment in cash (which should nearly always be questioned), or sudden absence of contact with an account that normally had lots of communication with you.

4. Reductions in merchandise, in the case of retailers, or any dramatic reduction in activity, in the case of other businesses.

Classification between major and minor receivables is also a good idea, since different approaches apply to probable conciliation court matters and to matters which are large enough to reach state or federal court in the event of your engaging in aggressive collection activity.

OTHER PRE-LAWSUIT CONSIDERATIONS

Once you have made a classification of the receivables between slow pay and bad debt, and between major and minor, there are some other considerations in dealing with debtors which should be borne in mind prior to even considering litigation.

Coercion Statutes

Nearly every state has a "coercion" statute. Briefly defined, coercion is threatening criminal prosecution in order to collect a debt or enhance one's position in a civil matter. Lawyers are sometimes guilty of this, and more often, unwitting creditors are guilty of coercion, which, in itself, is a crime. Don't let this be your mistake. If a debtor has committed a crime such as writing a no-account or NSF check to pay a debt to you, or committed something akin to criminal fraud in the process of becoming a debtor, never write to him or make a statement along the following lines: "If you don't pay up quickly, I'll have you thrown in jail," or, "Writing an NSF check is a crime in this state. If you don't make that check good by having that money in my hands by the close of business next Friday, I'll have you prosecuted for it." Both of the foregoing examples are clearly coercion. Perhaps you have already committed coercion. If so, you are fortunate to have not found yourself in serious legal trouble.

You are probably asking yourself at this point, "Well, suppose somebody does write an NSF check? What am I supposed to do, just let him get away with it?" We do not suggest anything of the kind. Just remember, however, that if you are going to do anything with the criminal authorities, it is separate from your civil remedies and should not be coupled with them. If you are going to turn someone in for writing an NSF check, simply do so without threatening to do it. If you wish to give the debtor an opportunity to make the check good, do so without mentioning its criminal aspects, and certainly without mentioning any threat to go to the criminal authorities with the check. There is nothing wrong with making a statement along the lines of: "I have an NSF check signed by you in my possession. I don't intend to do anything about it, provided you make it good by close of business next Friday." If the debtor asks you what you mean by "doing something about it" we recommend that you keep your answer vague such as, "I haven't determined what I'm going

to do about it, but I certainly will consider all my remedies."
Such statements are not coercion, since they do not mention
or imply criminal prosecution. This is not to say that you
cannot prosecute. What you cannot do is to threaten prosecution in order to collect.

Prosecutors vary in terms of how much they are willing to
act as "collection agencies." Most insist upon being able to
prosecute through to a conviction regardless of whether the
debtor makes restitution. In the authors' experience, however,
a plea bargain predicated upon an offer of full restitution by a
debtor frequently results in a dismissal of the charge or a
greatly reduced charge.

Bulk Sales Acts

Nearly every state has a bulk sales act. This is a statute
which provides that whenever a debtor sells substantially all
of his stock in trade, or other business property, without
paying his creditors on a pro rata basis, he is in violation of
the Bulk Sales Act for going out of business without taking
care of his trade accounts. In such a case, creditors who have
not been paid off have a right to set aside such sales so that all
the property of the business can be devoted to the benefit of all
of the creditors. Thus, in dealing with debtors, it is important
to make occasional visits to their business premises to see
whether they are selling off all of their stock in trade. If so,
bulk sales acts may provide some protection. This leads
naturally to the next subsection, bankruptcy.

Bankruptcy

As suggested in the preceding section, a violation of the
Bulk Sales Act may be an "act of bankruptcy" which would
also permit a filing of a bankruptcy petition against a debtor.
There are basically two kinds of bankruptcy—involuntary and
voluntary. Voluntary reorganizations are bankruptcies and are
governed by certain chapters of the United States Bankruptcy

Act, such as Chapters XI and XIII, where a debtor, realizing that he cannot pay his debts in the ordinary course of business, seeks an arrangement whereby he can stay in business, have an orderly disposition of his debts, and still remain in control. Involuntary bankruptcy, on the other hand, occurs when a debtor is hopelessly in debt, is not able to discharge his debts as they come due, and three of his creditors file a bankruptcy petition against him in order to force him into a liquidation of his business or some forced arrangement with his creditors. In either event—voluntary or involuntary bankruptcy—unless you have considerable experience in filing claims in bankruptcy, it is probably time to consult your faithful lawyer. Certainly, if you are going to file an involuntary bankruptcy petition against a debtor, you are going to require legal help. On the other hand, if you receive a notice of bankruptcy and a notice of time to file claims, and you have previously filed claims in bankruptcy, or even, perhaps, appeared at creditors' meetings at bankruptcies, you may very well be able to handle the filing of your claim yourself. More will be said about bankruptcy later in this section.

Private Arrangements as Alternatives to Bankruptcy

Oftentimes, it is more advantageous to make some private arrangement with a debtor, even if he happens to be technically insolvent, so that a bankruptcy petition could be filed against him. One good reason for making such a private arrangement is to get into a secured position, thereby obtaining a priority in the event of an eventual bankruptcy. If you have a debtor who owes you a substantial sum of money and you happen to be the creditor pressing him the hardest, he may well be willing to give you a security interest in some collateral that he has—such as a mortgage on land, a chattel mortgage on equipment, perhaps a sale and leaseback of equipment, or some other arrangement whereby you achieve a higher status in the event of bankruptcy than an unsecured creditor. If the debtor's business can survive the four months within which the Bankruptcy Act would make such an arrangement a voidable preferance as a matter of law, you will have substantially enhanced your position.

Further, debtors frequently prefer private arrangements with all of their creditors rather than going through the bankruptcy courts and gaining unwelcome publicity and creating expense which might be avoided. If you represent a major creditor of such a debtor, you should be certain to get in on the ground floor, probably as a member of a creditors' committee. If there is a substantial sum of money at stake, it is probably a good idea to consult your lawyer and get some form of credit-extension agreement drafted, protecting your interests. Under such arrangements, creditors frequently take assignments of the common stock of a corporation, get notes turned into convertible debentures (which are the equivalent of notes which can be turned into common stock in the event of default in a payment plan), make arrangements for sale of goods on consignment, and take other intelligent measures designed to protect themselves from losing at the hands of a business in trouble.

Careful consideration should be given as to whether such a private arrangement is preferable to a bankruptcy. Frequently it is, particularly in cases where you really trust the debtor and do not need the sanction of a court once he has agreed to go along with an arrangement. Such arrangements can be considerably more flexible than bankruptcies, and probably will result in your obtaining greater security than you might at the hands of a bankruptcy judge—if you are assertive enough to bargain for your rights and obtain security interests and other concessions.

COLLECTION LETTERS

Some collectors have made the drafting and sending of collection letters a fine art. Your prior classification of the account as slow pay or a bad debt or a probable-bad-debt should determine the form of collection letter you send. We recommend having at least three collection letters ready for use in your business: a "soft" letter, which is simply a reminder that an account has gone past due, to send to accounts which seem to be slow pay; a somewhat harder letter, to accounts which you suspect may become bad accounts or which have become chronic slow pay; and a "hard" letter, to those accounts about which you have very real concern. The "soft" letter might contain a message something like the following:

> Dear _____ :
>
> We note that your account has become .past due. Your credit rating is important in your dealings with us. Therefore, we felt it in your best interests to remind you how important it is for you to maintain your good credit rating with us by keeping this account current. Please forward your remittance no later than _____ . Thank you for promptly taking care of this matter.
>
> Very truly yours,

A somewhat firmer letter might be sent to a chronically slow account:

> Dear _____ :
>
> This letter is to notify you that your past due account in the amount of $ _____ can no longer be tolerated by our company. Your account is now _____ days overdue, is affecting your credit rating with us, and must be cleared up immediately. Please remit by return mail. Thank you.
>
> Very truly yours,

Finally, a "hard" letter, to those accounts which have shown danger signals:

> Dear _____ :
>
> PLEASE TAKE NOTICE that this is the last communication you will receive from our company before legal action is

instituted. You are hereby notified that unless your delinquent account in the amount of $ _____ is fully paid with our company by close of business, Friday, September _____ , 19 _____ , your account will be turned over to [our attorneys or a collection agency] for assertion of all of our legal remedies against you. We repeat: THIS IS THE LAST NOTICE YOU WILL RECEIVE BEFORE ACTION IS TAKEN AGAINST YOU. Please take care of this immediately!

Sincerely,

Hopefully, sending one of the foregoing letters will collect the account for you. If not, and you have sent the third letter, action is recommended. Nothing will destroy your credibility with your debtors more than threatening to take action and failing to do so.

"Account Stated"

One reason it is important to bill and send dunning notices or letters is to establish an "account stated" status for the account. An account stated is a legal concept which is applicable in nearly all United States jurisdictions. A simple definition of this concept is that once a creditor establishes that a debtor has received statements, or notices of the account he owes, and fails to raise an objection, the debtor loses his right to challenge the underlying basis for the debt. The way this works is that if you send billing notices to the debtor for services or merchandise, and if the debtor fails to make a reasonably prompt objection to the quality of the merchandise or services, he loses his right to so object, as well as the right to object to the amount of the bill. This reduces his potential defenses, in the event you have to go to court to collect the account, to only whether he has been properly identified as the debtor, whether he received the notices, etc. There is a legal presumption that when one mails something, it is received. Consequently, the importance of prompt, regular billing and collection letters cannot be overemphasized.

SUING DELINQUENT ACCOUNTS AND USE OF COLLECTION AGENCIES

A threshold consideration in taking a debtor to court is whether or not you wish to do it yourself or turn it over to a collection agency. If you are running a small business and have numerous bad accounts, you may very well be better off using a reputable collection agency. Caution should be exercised here; some collectors are so overly aggressive that they can expose their principals to lawsuits for abuse of legal process. We strongly recommend checking out the credentials of any collection agency employed to collect a debt before retaining them. Usually they have to be licensed at the state level. This is the first place to check to determine whether or not they are in any difficulty. We further recommend checking with your Better Business Bureau to determine whether there have been many complaints against an agency you are considering.

Finally, before retaining a collector, some direct questions should be asked. Do not be shy about this. Determine whether your collector's rates are competitive with other collection agencies. There is nothing wrong with doing some comparison shopping with regard to collectors. Further, you should be free to ask whether or not the collector you are hiring is bonded.

In addition to inquiring about rates or percentages, you should inquire where the collector will keep the money he collects for you, and how promptly he will remit to you. Some delay can normally be expected, to give time for checks that are collected from debtors to clear the bank. However, reputable collection agencies remit promptly on a regular basis. If you have a lot of accounts, cash flow can be important, and it should be determined how quickly your collector is going to remit to you. Once again, it is wise to make comparisons between the speed of remittance from various collectors. References are a good idea. Do not be hesitant to ask for them, and be certain to call some of them and check them out. If the agency is reputable, reasonable, and successful, it should be happy to provide you with some good references.

This is not to say that you should make no attempt at collecting accounts yourself before turning matters over to collectors. If you can collect accounts without resorting to collectors by simply having an orderly billing and collection-letter process, obviously, you save yourself the collector's fee. Further, if you have a regular procedure for sending accounts to collectors, such as accounts which have received your third collection letter and have still not paid, you should still retain the option of attempting to collect certain accounts yourself. For example, you may wish to retain major accounts that you want to sue immediately, and represent yourself or utilize a lawyer to sue, or you may wish to retain certain small accounts that are easy to collect in small claims court—once you have established to your own satisfaction that it pays to take certain claims to small claims court.

Once again, making the distinction between small and large claims and whether you are going to go to a small claims ("conciliation" court) or to a higher court is a good idea.

Conciliation Court

Conciliation, or small claims, courts are usually set up for appearances by lay people appearing without the assistance of an attorney. Indeed, some small claims courts have rules which prohibit attorneys from appearing in them. Others strongly discourage lawyers. The idea is that these are "people's courts" where small matters can be disposed of without resorting to costly legal process—including the cost of attorneys. Some complaints have arisen in recent years over whether the small claims courts are really for the people or whether they are for collection agencies. Commonly, a small claims docket is full of collectors coming to get small claims court judgments against debtors, with only a smattering of private disputes. Whether or not this is a good thing is a subject for debate and will not be addressed here except to state in passing that if the collectors were not able to go to small claims court, they would undoubtedly go to higher courts, which would mean that additional court costs and fees would get taxed against debtors by collection agencies.

Some small claims courts get around the problem of over-crowded dockets by having a separate docket devoted to collection agencies, and the remainder of the time devoted to the disputes, claims, and accounts of private individuals and businesses. In any event, the procedures are usually simplified; clerks are normally helpful; and a call to the courthouse and a visit to the small claims court office will provide you with all the information necessary to file a claim and get a judgment.

Typically, conciliation court judgments, like the summons and complaints, are simply mailed to defendants. In order to send the sheriff out to collect a conciliation court judgment, in most jurisdictions it is necessary to take another step: one must take the conciliation court judgment to a court of higher jurisdiction, most typically a municipal court, in order to get a municipal court judgment entered upon the conciliation court judgment. The concept of volunteerism in payment and showing up in conciliation court, blended with the American jurisprudential concept of adequate notice and hearing, is what necessitates this extra step, which seems rather superflu-ous to many. In any event, once you have a conciliation court judgment, you should be certain to check with the clerk of conciliation court to determine what steps are necessary, if any, to obtain a writ of *execution* sending a sheriff out to execute your judgment for you.

If you are baffled, once again it is time to consult your attorney. Indeed, in some instances, it may be necessary to obtain the services of an attorney in order to get the concilia-tion court judgment transformed into a judgment which can be utilized for activity by the sheriff. If you are a businessman who regularly uses the conciliation court, one way to cut down expense is to wait until you have a number of judg-ments and then send them to your attorney in batches.

COLLECTING A JUDGMENT

There are several means whereby judgments can be collected:

Execution

This is mentioned in the preceding subsection. Basically, a "writ of execution" is a court order commanding the sheriff to go to the residence or place of business of the debtor and *levy* execution upon the debtor or any of his property by making a demand upon the debtor and seizing and taking away any property the debtor has which is not exempt by statute. Exempt property which cannot be levied upon is, normally, the debtor's homestead, personal effects, and work tools, as spelled out by state statute. Most sheriffs are knowledgeable about what property is exempt under the law of their state. Once the sheriff has seized property, as opposed to obtaining money by demand, it is returned by the sheriff to a bonded sheriff's warehouse for later sale at public auction or by other means specified by statute. Once the cost of storage and sheriff's fees for levying and execution are deducted, the remainder can be used to satisfy the judgment. Any excess is returned to the debtor. Care should be taken in designating property to be seized by the sheriff that the costs of seizing, storing, and sale do not exceed the value of the property. If so, the creditor who sends the sheriff out on such a mission will experience the pain of catching nothing, plus having to stand the sheriff's costs!

Attachment

Attachment is a document which, when served upon the holder of the property of a debtor, requires him to hold it for the eventuality of seizure, sale, and utilization to satisfy a judgment. Normally, property which is attached is in the hands of a third party, but occasionally property is attached in the hands of the debtor himself. Normally, once an attachment has been made on property, if the property considerably exceeds the judgment, the debtor finds a way to pay the judgment rather than having the property sold at a distress sale to satisfy the judgment. The same usually happens when the sheriff levies execution upon property of a value substantially in excess of the amount of the judgment.

Garnishment

Garnishment is sending a garnishment summons to a bank or employer or other person owing money to the debtor. Frequently it is used against wage earners. Most states have statutes specifying the percentage of the debtor's wages which can be garnisheed. Garnishment merely requires the employer, bank, or other person to hold the garnisheed sums. In order to get the garnisheed sums applied to the debt, one has to levy execution in most instances.

Supplementary Proceedings, or "Proceedings Subsequent"

Supplementary proceedings, or "proceedings subsequent," are little hearings which are conducted before a magistrate, judge, or a court reporter empowered to put the debtor under oath for questioning. Basically, what happens in such proceedings is that the debtor receives a summons which requires him, under force of law, to appear before such a magistrate, judge, or court reporter, to answer questions under oath as to the extent and location of his assets. Once this is learned, the sheriff can be sent out to levy execution. Such proceedings are a great annoyance and embarrassment, and frequently, upon receipt of a summons for supplementary proceedings, debtors pay up. Further, by going through an exhaustive list of potential sources of nonexempt property, one usually finds some property that can be levied upon, such as sporting goods and other items that may not have much value but which are dear to the heart of the debtor. Once such property is discovered, it is amazing how often debtors come up with "relatives and friends" or other sources to pay the judgment.

All of the foregoing remedies for collecting judgments can be performed by laymen, but more commonly they are performed by attorneys on behalf of creditors.

Litigation of large claims is normally left in the hands of attorneys if there are substantial, complicated defenses. However, laymen are fully capable of handling many lawsuits. If you are so disposed, the authors recommend *How to Handle Your Own Lawsuit,* by Jerome S. Rice (Chicago: Contemporary Books, Inc., 1979). This book is a valuable, step-by-step guide for the layman who wishes to represent himself in court.

REMEDIES OF SECURED CREDITORS

If you have been fortunate enough to obtain a *security interest,* such as a security interest in personal property or fixtures (under Article 9 of the Uniform Commercial Code, which has been enacted by most states) or in the accounts of a debtor or contracts for deed or other *chattel paper* or other goods (such as consumer goods, equipment, farm products, or inventory) and have perfected it by having the debtor sign a written security agreement and have made appropriate filings or have taken possession of the collateral upon the default of the debtor, you generally have authority to seize and dispose of the collateral in the most profitable way, thus maximizing the amount available to pay the debt to you and any other unpaid obligations of the debtor. The Uniform Commercial Code simply requires that such disposition be "commercially reasonable." Further, if you have a mortgage on real estate, there are steps which can be taken to foreclose, which your attorney knows about.

If you do succeed in liquidating a security interest, normally there are statutes which allow the debtor to redeem the collateral before the secured party has disposed of it, entered into a contract to dispose of it, or obtained the right to retain the collateral to satisfy the obligation. The redeeming party, however, must pay all obligations secured by the collateral, including the expenses involved in repossessing, preparing the collateral for sale, and, if provided in a valid security agreement, reasonable attorney's fees and legal expenses involved in seizing it.

Care should be taken to seize and dispose of property in accordance with the law, since penalties can be assessed against people who wrongfully seize and dispose of collateral without having perfected a security interest, or before there is a true default.

BULK TRANSFERS

A bulk transfer is any transfer in bulk, not in the ordinary course of the debtor's business, of a major part of the materials, supplies, merchandise, or other inventory of his enterprise. Normally, "major" has been defined as meaning more than 50 percent. Laws in some states substitute the word "substantial" for "major," which has been determined to be as low as 5 percent of the transferor's total inventory in a California case. Nearly all businesses involved in the sale of merchandise from stock, including those who manufacture what they sell, are subject to bulk sales provisions. If a debtor makes such an unlawful bulk transfer, the transferor must, upon determination that the transfer is a bulk transfer, furnish a list of his creditors and cooperate with an auctioneer or other seller in preparation of a schedule of his property. The auctioneer then normally gets the list of creditors, give notice of sale to all creditors listed, holds the sale, and satisfies the creditors out of the net proceeds of the auction. Thus, if you have a deadbeat who is trying to get out of paying his debts by closing down his business and selling everything off outside of the ordinary course of business, there is a powerful remedy in the bulk sales act of most states.

LIENS

The most common *lien* is the "mechanic's lien," enacted to provide a remedy for laborers, materialmen, contractors or subcontractors who are unable to collect for their contribution to the construction or improvement of real estate. In addition, there are attorney's liens upon papers and property of their clients, liens protecting persons who repair automobiles, sometimes called "garagemen's" liens, and many other liens created by statute. All lien laws are creatures of statute, and permit creditors, under the appropriate circumstances, to obtain security interests in property which they have improved. Following the statutory procedure, such security interests can be foreclosed upon, and the proceeds used to satisfy the lien. In many states, landlords have liens on the property of their tenants, or on the premises.

Usually, the procedures for foreclosure require notification of all other persons with recorded security interests and other persons in possession of the premises or of whom the lienholder has knowledge. There are time limits, such as ninety days in Minnesota, for the filing of a mechanic's lien which starts running upon the completion of the last item of work. Care should be taken in determining the exact time limits involved for the filing and for commencement of foreclosure of such liens; otherwise, the lienholder's rights to the lien are lost.

Sometimes, lawsuits are fought over who has priority among mechanic's lien claimants, mortgagees, and holders of other security interests. Normally, such litigation is very complex and should not be left to amateurs.

Other liens not previously mentioned, which some statutes provide for, and which can be the subject matter of such disputes are the following: liens for government services; hospital charges; liens of commissioners of public welfare; liens of county boards for hospital fees; innkeepers' and hotel keepers' liens; breeders' liens on the offspring from stud horses, bulls, etc.; laborers' liens protecting employees of manufacturers, merchants, or dealers in merchandise; launderers' liens; liens on logs and timber for manual labor concerning it; liens for processing farm products, shoeing animals; liens of veterinarians; liens of warehousemen and carriers; which include demurrage and terminal charges; and any other lien that the legislature of a particular state may have thought up. As you can see, the entire area of lien law can be exceedingly complex.

MECHANICS OF BANKRUPTCY CLAIMS

Bankruptcy is a very specialized system of jurisprudence. The primary purpose of the Bankruptcy Act is to collect and distribute the assets of a bankrupt, or insolvent person, for the benefit of his creditors, to the fullest extent, without doing injury to the rights of the individual or a class of creditors. A secondary purpose is to grant a discharge from obligations in order to give an honest debtor a fresh start.

As stated previously, bankruptcy can be broken down between voluntary and involuntary bankruptcy. In voluntary bankruptcy, any person (except a municipal, railroad, insurance, or banking corporation, or building and loan association) can voluntarily petition to be adjudged bankrupt. The filing of an involuntary petition institutes an action requiring a judgment by a referee in bankruptcy, who handles proceedings before him as bankruptcy judge.

Involuntary bankruptcy can be obtained against any natural person (except a wage earner or farmer) and against any monied business or commercial corporation (except a building and loan association; municipal, railroad, insurance, or banking corporation) owing more than $1,000. It can be commenced by a petition filed by three or more creditors with provable claims amounting to $500 in excess of the value of any security held by them. If the total number of creditors is less than twelve, then one or more creditors whose provable claims equal that amount can file the petition. Specifically, the petition must allege, and the petitioner must be prepared to prove, that the debtor has done certain acts in bankruptcy, such as the following:

1. Has concealed, or removed, or permitted concealment or removal of, any part of his property with intend to hinder, defraud, or delay creditors, or made some other "fraudulent transfer" as defined by statute.

2. Has made a preferential transfer as defined by statute, preferring one or more of his creditors over the others.

3. Has allowed, while insolvent, any creditor to obtain a lien on property and has failed to have it vacated or discharged within thirty days after the lien.

4. Has made a general assignment for the benefit of his creditors.

5. Has obtained, while insolvent, the appointment of a receiver or trustee to take charge of his property.

6. Has admitted in writing his inability to pay his debts and his willingness to be adjudicated as a bankrupt.

Other sections within the bankruptcy statutes permit wage earner plans, bankruptcy of farmers, savings and loans, banks, railroads, insurance corporations, etc. All of them are similar in purpose.

Once the proceedings are started, the bankruptcy court has exclusive jurisdiction over all property of the bankrupt that is in the actual or constructive control of the bankrupt at the time the petition is filed. Once the bankruptcy has started, liens cannot be acquired, and no other court has the power to attach, seize, or fix a lien, or in any way reach the property. Further, once the bankruptcy has started, it acts as an automatic stay of any lawsuit or action—and of the commencement or continuance of any action or court proceeding—to enforce any rights against the debtor.

The bankrupt has numerous duties, including the following: to attend the first meeting of creditors, who are all notified; to comply with all lawful orders of the court; to submit to examination by (and to report to) the trustee who is appointed, concerning the correctness of various proofs of claim which are filed by the creditors; to execute and deliver such papers as ordered by the court; to execute and deliver conveyances and transfers of property in foreign countries; to inform the trustee of any attempts by creditors or other persons to evade the act; to report any knowledge of anybody attempting to prove a false claim; to prepare and file (under oath) a schedule of property, a list of creditors, and any claims for exemptions; to prepare and file a statement of his affairs; to prepare and file a detailed inventory of merchandise or other property when required; to file a statement of all contracts that are in the process of being executed; and to generally cooperate with the trustee in the preparation of the inventory, examination of claims, and administration of the disposition of all assets and debts.

The trustee is appointed at the first meeting of creditors, and is usually a person knowledgeable in the affairs of persons such as the debtor, and in dispositions of the estates of the bankrupt. The trustee has to file a bond, and is normally elected by a majority vote of the creditors.

Exemptions

The bankrupt is allowed to retain some property free from the claim of the trustee, but such a claim to exemptions must be affirmatively asserted by the bankrupt. If the bankrupt fails to claim the exemptions, his spouse, dependent children, or other qualified person can file a claim for him. The state of domicile determines the exemptions not provided for by the bankruptcy and other laws of the United States. The most common exemptions are the homestead of the debtor, life insurance death benefits, wages and miscellaneous personal property, including tools of trade. Title to such exempt property does not pass to the court or vest in the trustee, but, rather, remains the bankrupt's. Conversions of nonexempt property, in an attempt to defeat creditors, into exempt property on the eve of bankruptcy can be "fraudulent" and such conversion can be set aside. Further, fraud on the part of the bankrupt that causes a creditor to lose money, if proved, will survive bankruptcy and cannot be discharged by the bankrupt.

"Fraudulent Acts"

Voluntary transfers by the bankrupt are declared fraudulent (under Section 67d(2) of the Bankruptcy Act)—including every transfer or obligation incurred by a debtor *within one year* prior to the filing of the bankruptcy petition, as to creditors existing at the time of such transfer or obligation—if such transfer was made without fair consideration by an insolvent debtor, or a debtor who made himself insolvent by making such a transfer or obligation, or if the transfer leaves the debtor with unreasonably small capital to run his business. As to existing and future creditors, a transfer or obligation is fraudulent if made without fair consideration by a debtor who intends to incur, or believes he will incur, debts beyond his ability to pay, or with an intent to hinder, delay, or defraud either existing or future creditors.

Naturally, the foregoing criteria require proof. This is what bankruptcy litigation is all about.

Further, every transfer made and every obligation incurred *within four months* preceding the filing of a petition by the debtor who is or will thereby be made insolvent, is fraudulent as to creditors then existing or future creditors, if such transfers or obligations were made or incurred in contemplation of filing a bankruptcy petition, or in order to give one class of creditors or one creditor a greater percentage of the debt owed them and if the transferee or person receiving the benefit of such a transaction knew or believed that the debtor intended to make such use of it.

Further, every transfer of partnership property or obligations incurred *within one year* prior to filing a petition in bankruptcy (when the partnership is insolvent or will thereby be rendered insolvent) is fraudulent, if made to a partner, or to a person not a partner but without fair consideration to the partnership.

All the foregoing voluntary and involuntary transfers or obligations are "fraudulent" by statutory definition in the Bankruptcy Act and will be set aside, and the property so transferred will go into the "pot" for the benefit of all general creditors.

Once the bankrupt estate is determined, by accumulating all of the debts of the bankrupt, the litigation in the bankruptcy court proceeds to consider whether or not there have been voidable preferences for certain people, and to establish priority of classes of creditors. Generally the priorities of classes of creditors run as follows:

1. First priority goes to costs and expenses of administration, referees' salaries, filing fees, trustees' expenses, fees and mileage paid to witnesses, and one reasonable attorney's fee.

2. Second priority goes to wages and commissions, not to exceed $600, earned within three months before the date of commencement of the bankruptcy, by workmen, servants, clerks, or sales people on either a salary or commission basis.

3. Third priority is for costs and expenses of creditors whose efforts result in refusal, revocation, or setting aside of an arrangement or wage earner plan, or in the bankrupt's discharge, or the conviction of a bankrupt of an offense under the bankruptcy laws.

4. Fourth priority goes to taxes owed to the United States or any state, not released by discharge in bankruptcy.

5. Fifth priority goes to the debts, other than taxes, owed to any person who, by the laws of the United States, is entitled to a priority and rent owed to a landlord entitled to priority under applicable state law.

Of course, *ahead of all of these priorities are security interests,* such as mortgages, chattel mortgages, etc., once it is established that they were validly incurred prior to the time periods set forth with regard to voluntary and involuntary transfers and obligations. Once again, one sees how important it is to *get into a secured position with a debtor as early as possible.*

5

Purchase and Sale of a Business

Many businessmen find themselves at one time or another involved as buyer or seller of a business, either as executives of purchasers or sellers, private investors, or the person who has built a business and is ready to translate his gains into cash or stock through sale or merger. This outline is not intended to be a guidebook but is intended to provide some warnings and some helpful comments on major questions that come up often enough in such transactions to warrant comment. There are not very many so-called routine matters in connection with these transactions, and we have left those to the lawyers in the deal. These comments are aimed at the businessman in relationship to the deal, what he should look out for, what he should expect from his lawyers, how he can make a better deal.

While it is apparently true that the first time U.S. Steel was sold, seventy-odd years ago, it was done on the back of a napkin in the recesses of a private club, this approach is not recommended for the rest of us. Today lawyers have to be involved, and should be expected to carry the burden of a transaction. Do not turn the deal over to your tax accountant. Tax considerations are important but should be weighed as part of the overall planning process because there are inevitable trade-offs between tax benefits and corporate and other advantages. It is generally good advice to say "bring your lawyer into the transaction early" so that you will not commit yourself to a cash-for-stock transaction in the first negotiating session with the seller, only to find out later that a tax-free deal involving stock for stock or a merger would have saved you a lot of money. It is very difficult for a lawyer to go hat in hand requesting that the deal be renegotiated in a different form, explaining that the client did not really mean what he said in the first go-around. If initial meetings must take place, and they frequently do, without the benefit of counsel, then confine them to matters of price and, perhaps, terms, leaving the structure of the deal to the lawyers.

Lawyers have, on occasion, earned the reputation of "Jack-the-deal killers." Clients tend to become very impatient as the negotiations drag on through several drafts of the agreement. The client should try to have a feel for whether *his* lawyer or *the other* lawyer is playing the role of deal killer by overdoing the nit-picking. If this becomes apparent, it is time for the principals to intervene—either by direct involvement with one another or through their lawyers—to head off this possibility. By the same token, delays do not necessarily mean frivolity. There are many important aspects of the language in a purchase agreement which will come back to haunt you later if not carefully dealt with at the outset. Ask your counsel for an explanation of why the issues that he is pressing are important, and he will usually be able to give you a pretty good reason. If not, the discussion will help to clarify his thinking about the importance of the point he is pressing in the context of the overall deal. The client will frequently have to be the final arbiter of questions about risk-taking on difficult issues. Attractive as it may seem to simply say, "I'm turning this deal over to you, Joe; negotiate the deal and let me know what I am supposed to sign," the lawyer is seldom in as good a position as the businessman to evaluate the importance of alternative forms of *guarantee language* on the collectibility of accounts receivable as opposed to the way in which this particular transaction will benefit some larger plan, or to appreciate that the total purchase price is such a bargain that it can tolerate a few losses later on.

By all means, use a lawyer with a lot of experience in the acquisition field. Avoid "Jack-the-deal killer" types. It is very easy to find ways to break a deal; much more creativity and effort is required to find ways to enable the parties to make a deal. The lawyer should constantly be able to offer alternative solutions to apparent impasses in the negotiating process. The experienced lawyer has seen a number of different ways to handle each major issue and should be prepared to try them out in an effort to bridge the gap. If, after that effort has been made, the parties are still apart due to basic differences, that is the time to recognize the effort is a bad job, shake hands, and part friends, knowing a good-faith effort has been made to explore the possible areas of agreement, but without success.

Once the initial contact has been made and the negotiations have started, the parties begin to circle one another with the wariness of tundra wolves. Rare it is that the first offer made is the one finally allowed or the one accepted. It is crucial to the ultimate outcome how the parties conduct themselves in the negotiating process. This is an art that cannot be learned by studying a set of rigid rules. It must be practiced. It is innate in a person to a large degree. Success comes more from the negotiator's character and experience than from tricks of the trade. There are, however, a few things that can be said about negotiating that are helpful.

One thing that studies of the negotiating process have shown is the importance of providing the other party with reasons to believe that he should accept your position and feel good about it. This approach can be contrasted with the non-negotiable demand approach, or the "I'm tougher than you can ever be" approach, in negotiating. Be persuasive, try to show the other fellow how he is better off with your proposal and that he has no choice but to consider the arguments which you are putting to him.

Closely related to this proposition is the one that your credibility must be based on evidence and sincerity. Use of an uncomfortable or unnatural negotiating style will inhibit your ability to exude credibility. If you are comfortable making gambits that lead to blind alleys simply as a negotiating ploy, so be it. If you are not, don't use them. It is important for the other fellow to believe that you are pursuing a fair deal by reflecting your important interests, rather than just negotiating for points. If he believes what you say, when you say it, the process will go much more smoothly.

This does not mean absolute candor on all issues. Absolute candor will simply generate a less than favorable deal for you in most cases. Resolution of this apparent dilemma is where the artistry in negotiating comes in. Before beginning the negotiation, it is often useful to have in your mind, or even on paper in outline form, what your ultimate objective is, and what stages of negotiation you can anticipate. The authors find it very useful in preparing for a negotiation to picture in their minds the dialogue between the parties on various important points. With enough experience, you can anticipate the responses to most of your proposals. This helps to clarify, refine, and change the proposal, in the first instance, and to avoid making a proposal that will shortly become untenable in the face of attacks by the other side. This also permits one to make use of psychological ploys.

The introduction of a particular point that would have been jarring if made earlier is frequently possible after two other points have been made. The imaginary envisioning of the opponent's responses and reactions to your proposals will give you a sense of the order of attack.

The use of questioning to seek information can frequently be used later in the process to one's advantage. Take this example: The purchaser is buying assets, but whether liabilities will be kept by the seller or assumed by the buyer is unresolved. The buyer has taken the position that the seller's liabilities look substantial, and he doesn't want to assume them. The seller then goes to great lengths to convince the buyer that the exposure is small. With a little guidance, the sellers can finally be jockied into putting a very low estimated dollar value on the liabilities. The trap can now be sprung. The buyer increases the purchase price by the estimated value of the liabilities and lets the seller keep them. Since the seller priced them, he's hard pressed to turn the offer down.

Don't let your ego get in the way of the ultimate objective— a good deal. A need to be a "winning" negotiator or a need to dominate the other fellow in the negotiating process can cost you a lot of money in the end. It is not necessary to insist on driving the car when you can sit in the back seat and tell the driver where to go.

However, whatever your technique, do not become a follower. Subtle control of the process is important. This comes out in such matters as who prepares the first draft of the agreement. Frequently, the client's first reaction is, let the other fellow's lawyer do it because then he will have to pay for it. This is fine, unless your lawyer never recovers the ground lost in that first draft. In that case, you may end up paying far more than the other fellow's lawyer's fees in the overall cost of the deal. It is generally advisable to get the right to prepare the first draft. This draft casts the structure of the deal; and that, alone, can be significant. Furthermore, the language changes that are subsequently made, if not complete, will leave you with some language that is advantageous. Either oversight on the other fellow's part or trade-offs against changes he requests in other areas can help you retain the language advantages you may gain by writing the first draft. It is oftentimes said to be traditional for the buyer's counsel to do the first draft, but this is not an inviolate rule, and the matter is certainly open to discussion during the process.

Another significant control technique is to produce the first agenda and timetable. While it can be presented as a draft for discussion purposes, it will establish the steps and procedures that will be followed in terms of meetings, the parties involved in meetings, where the meetings will take place, when and if there will be investigations by auditors, by lawyers, by others, and so on. When approaching a major negotiating session or meeting, sit down with your team and identify a few very specific objectives for that meeting. This is useful even if the meeting is an informational one. Exactly what do you want to accomplish at the meeting? If this can be put in writing, it will help to focus your thinking. Many meetings simply ramble off in general discussions; but the person who is zeroing in on a particular goal will get more of what he wants than the fellow who does not.

Another element of control is a letter of intent preliminary to the definitive agreement. Letters of intent are important and useful when the buyer or the seller feels the other party is shaky in his commitment to the deal, even though the handshake stage has been reached. If the buyer is afraid the seller will turn around and sell to someone else before a binding agreement can be signed, then he will press for a letter of intent summarizing the substantive points of the deal, such as price, terms, even the form of the deal—whether it is for cash, notes, stock, or otherwise. This also provides an opportunity to sneak up on some of the warranty issues and closing issues that will arise in the definitive agreement by summarizing a list of usual and customary representations and warranties to be included in the definitive agreement. One can throw into the letter of intent assurances on accounts receivable, the accuracy of financial statements, warranty of the salability of equipment, patents, trademarks, of noninfringement of patents and trademarks, which may not solicit cries of anguish from the other side in the context of a letter of intent, but would if raised later on. Once they are in the letter of intent, you have a basis for insisting that they go into the definitive agreement.

Letters of intent can be binding or nonbinding. If they are silent on the subject and spell out all of the substantive terms of the deal, such as the price, terms, and the like, they are probably binding. If they do not do so, but constitute an agreement to agree at a later date, they are probably not binding. The buyer faced with a shifting or nervous seller will push for a binding letter of intent that states that the terms spelled out in the letter of intent are binding on the parties and may not be renegotiated, but, nonetheless, additional customary representations and warranties and related agreements will be the subject of the definitive agreement to be prepared by the parties thereafter. This permits a two-stage negotiation, wherein the deal is negotiated and nailed down and stated to be not renegotiable at the second stage. The second stage is then the definitive agreement negotiation, which is limited to the terms not previously set in the letter of intent. Without such a limitation, the definitive agreement stage often becomes a renegotiation of the price.

On the other hand if the buyer is fairly confident about the seller's willingness to go through with the deal and is really more concerned about his own ability to investigate the business before finally signing on the dotted line, he will want a nonbinding letter of intent. From our experience it is quite unusual for a truly binding letter of intent to be signed. Too many issues remain open between the parties at that stage to permit anyone to be comfortable with that approach. Nonetheless, we have found it useful on some occasions.

Another factor in the letter of intent stage is worth mentioning. Once a public announcement is made that a deal has been struck, both parties have limited their options. More importantly the seller has locked himself in with respect to the possibility of selling to other people. His options are much more restricted. If the buyer subsequently backs away from the deal and announces that he has done so, the rest of the world will see the business as tainted merchandise. The question will always hover in the air, "Why did that buyer back out after he had made a close investigation of the business? What did he discover that I don't know?" The savvy seller will be aware of this danger and try to avoid public announcements if he is big enough for that kind of announcement to be noticeable in the business community.

When public companies are involved, the general rule of thumb is that the securities laws and the Securities and Exchange Commission require a public announcement at the letter of intent stage. This is not always honored but is followed by many securities lawyers. Consequently, public company deals oftentimes will not involve a letter of intent, which would put them in the position of having to make a public announcement. Control of the public announcement should be agreed upon between the parties if one is concerned about premature public announcements. It is not enough to be silent on the subject if you are afraid the other fellow will make the announcement and thereby box you in. Require that mutual agreement be reached before any announcement can be made, and that then the announcement will be a joint one.

COMPROMISE

Compromise is the central aspect of any negotiation. Both parties want to make a deal or they wouldn't be sitting down together. In order to maximize the chances of the deal happening, one must be prepared to compromise. This is particularly true when the buyer and seller will have to live together on some basis after the closing. A little money given up on the purchase price may pay great dividends in the willingness of the seller to assist in the later management of the business.

It is useful in some cases to know how to say no without seeming negative or slamming the door. If the other side wants to omit any representation concerning the seller's qualification to do business in other states, you reply: "We always insist on such a representation, but we will be happy to listen to your arguments as to why it is necessary in your particular situation." The burden is then on him to persuade you, but you are not agreeing to anything, only assuming the pose of the reasonable person willing to listen to reasonable argument. When he is done making his arguments you say, "While I am not entirely persuaded, I will certainly consider it with my counsel and let you know our response." By the end of the discussion or the end of the meeting, you have given up absolutely nothing, but the other side has not been slapped in the face.

Bear in mind as the negotiation progresses the need to establish a consistent or credible position and image that will bear fruit in the end. For example, in the process of negotiation a number of issues will arise involving questions such as, "Is the value of this asset $50,000 or $100,000?" One party will want an indemnification against undisclosed potential product liability claims; and the other party will want a hold harmless on personal guarantees of loans. A negotiator who resolves each of these issues—by splitting the difference at $75,000 in the one case or by trading off the two apparently symmetrical representations in the other—will not be in nearly as strong a position by the end of the negotiation as the fellow who handles each of those issues carefully and concretely, who treats each issue as a matter of reasoned analysis, not of horse trading.

A fellow who can marshal facts to show that his claim that a machine is worth $50,000 is based on an analysis of its depreciated value, its remaining useful life, and the number of widgets it will produce during the balance of its remaining life; who can argue that the need for indemnity on product liabilities is far more pressing because of three claims of increasing severity made over the last three years, coupled with his knowledge that the seller considered a recall six months ago and has been experiencing a high level of warranty claims for defective products, will be a far more formidable bargainer than the horse trader. The pattern of reasoned analysis in support of each position throughout the negotiation, followed by a little rapid horse trading to bridge the last gap in the transaction, can be a very useful mix of techniques, but not in the reverse order.

A word about persistence is appropriate. Many a negotiation has finally been won by the fellow who is able to doggedly keep at the transaction without blowing his cool, who can be alert, reasonable, and consistent at two o'clock in the morning in the third week of negotiation. Lots of people can sit down for a day's worth of negotiating and calmly consider the prospect of dancing around the issues until ten or eleven o'clock at night. When the room gets stuffy and nerves get frazzled, people get tired, but they don't necessarily go home. A person who is alert and tough-minded after midnight will frequently break the negotiations wide open to his advantage. Negotiations generate their own compulsions. The longer a negotiation lasts and the further it progresses, the more it tends to make people want to make a deal simply because they have spent so much time attempting to do so. There is a certain wish to avoid the failure that goes with not consummating their desired goal. This can be useful or it can be harmful. The danger lies in making a deal for the sake of a deal, even when it is not a good one. Be aware when minor issues have assumed major importance in the negotiations. Don't fall into the trap of treating them as major issues in your own mind. Be prepared to take advantage of the lack of perspective on the other side, and you will be a long step ahead of the other fellow.

6

Buy-Sell Agreements *or* How to Avoid Widows in Board Rooms

REASONS FOR BUY-SELL AGREEMENTS

In a closed corporation with a few principal shareholders, the character of the partners in the business is crucial to the success of the business and to their ability to get along. Since, under the law, stock is freely transferable, a specific contract is required to create desired restrictions on transfer. The partners in the business want to know who is going to step into their respective shoes once they leave the business by means of death, disability, or termination. Widows and orphans in board rooms can be very troublesome. Consequently, thought should be given at an early stage to whether someone's son, daughter, or widow is wanted in the business after good old Joe has gone away. Normally, agreement is reached about what happens to the stock upon the occurrence of one of the triggering events.

Another reason for a buy-sell agreement is to provide a

market for the stock if it is not publicly traded. This means that if an acceptable outside buyer cannot be found, then one of the other owners of the company must buy the stock, or the company itself must buy it. Two important considerations in selecting among these alternatives are tax planning and ability to finance the buy out.

TRIGGER EVENTS

The buy-sell agreement can provide for a number of trigger events that will have the effect of giving one party or the other the right to buy or sell the stock. Typically, the death of one of the stockholders will give the remaining stockholders or the corporation the right to buy the stock from the estate. The correlative right of the estate to require the remaining stockholders or the corporation to buy the stock goes hand-in-hand with their right to buy from the estate. Death, disability (as determined by a physician appointed by the corporation, for example), incompetence (as determined by a court, for example), termination of employment, bankruptcy, assignment for the benefit of creditors or the receipt of a bona fide offer from a third party are all triggering events that may be included in an agreement.

In the case of a third-party offer provision, the shareholder who wants to get out before the occurrence of one of the other, rather final, events described above, can do so. He can find a buyer for his stock, but under the buy-sell agreement, he must first offer it to the corporation or his other partners at either a prearranged price or at the price offered by the third party. It is important to require that the third-party offer be bona fide and *arms length,* so as to prevent a phony trigger at a low price. In most cases, the proposition that the other parties to the buy-sell must meet a bona fide third-party offer will provide the closest approximation to true market value of the property. However, this approach may not be the most acceptable among the group. They have no way of knowing in advance what the offer may look like, and it may come at an awkward time. The establishment of a price agreeable to all of them may make outside sales more difficult, but it will facilitate sales within the group.

PRICE FORMULAS

Consequently, it is often the best approach to set a stipulated value for the stock, which is agreed upon by all parties, or some high percentage of the parties, to the buy-sell agreement. The stipulated price can be effective until a new price is adopted; however, if no stipulated price has been set within twelve months before the trigger event, then the value can be set by a formula or an appraisal. The requirement that the parties agree to a stipulated value is calculated to produce a value most likely to be acceptable to all parties to the agreement. Likewise the exercise of establishing the value will force the parties to think fairly about the price, and should induce them to talk to their lawyer, their accountant, or other financial adviser about the value of their business. Once this has been done, subsequent annual valuations are not nearly as difficult. In some businesses, such as insurance agencies and banks, there are well-known formulas typically followed that can be used instead of a stipulated value. For example, buy-sell agreements for small banks in the Midwest would typically be at 1¼ to 1¾ times *book value* (including half or all of the loan loss reserves in the book value). In the Rocky Mountain states, the value is more likely to be twice book, with various adjustments. Insurance agencies seem to sell for 1½ to 2 times annual commissions, and so on.

Appraisals are a cumbersome method which should be used only as a last resort. They are time consuming and expensive, and not necessarily satisfactory, unless the parties have only a vague idea of what their company is worth or unless they are feuding so badly that an agreement is impossible. Then an outsider is necessary and should be provided for. There are companies that offer this kind of service. A full-blown appraisal of a medium size business will cost $10,000 to $20,000.

Smaller businesses can be handled by less formal means at significantly lower fees. One approach for a full-blown problem appraisal is to permit each party to the buy-sell agreement to appoint one appraiser and the two appraisers, so appointed, shall, within ten days after their designation, jointly designate a third appraiser and notify the parties of his identity. If they cannot agree on the third appraiser, then a petition to the local court can be filed by them, and the agreement can authorize the court to appoint the third appraiser. Variation on this theme can consist of a limitation that the appraisers shall in no event determine a value lower than that contained in a bona fide written offer submitted within ninety days of the triggering event.

If book value or a multiple of earnings formula is to be used, take care to specify the treatment of the period between fiscal years. The cost of having accountants prepare interim statements can be significant and should be taken into consideration. It normally saves money to specify that the company's regular accountant shall provide the stub period statements, if required. If insurance is purchased to fund the buy-sell agreement, the proceeds of the policy should be excluded from the value of the company in computing the book value thereof. Otherwise, an inflated number will be derived, and the benefit of the insurance lost.

PAYMENT

Typically, the payment terms will provide for a down payment of 10 percent to 29 percent, and the balance will be paid over a period of years at an interest rate fluctuating with the prime rate of a designated bank. Depending on the riskiness of the business, it may be *at* prime, or one, two, or three points above prime. Frequently, the promissory note delivered for the stock is secured by a pledge of the stock certificates until the note is paid off. A prepayment provision should be dealt with in case the buyer is able to refinance with a lender or does not need a period of time to make the payments. If insurance is purchased to fund the buy-sell agreement, the agreement itself should identify the insurance and clearly assign the rights of ownership to the corporation or other parties, if that is the case, and provide for the payment of the proceeds as agreed. If it has incurred the obligation to make more than one stock purchase under the buy-sell agreement, provision should be made to permit the corporation to stretch out the payments. Likewise, if there are insufficient corporate funds, a provision should be made for the treatment of the obligation in this case. Most state, corporate laws require the existence of capital or earned surplus equal to the redemption price before stock can be redeemed. The reason for this provision is to protect creditors of the corporation. If this is the case, the remaining shareholders may be called upon to make the payments, and to consent to the redemption or forgo it. The interest rate on the redemption obligation should preferably be tied to some kind of a floating rate. Fixed rates are risky in light of this country's last thirty years' experience with interest rates. The average interest rate charged by banks to their prime customers has steadily risen and can be expected to continue to do so in the near future.

Company *versus* Personal Agreements

Buy-sell agreements can either be among individuals or between individuals and the company they own. Under the existing tax law, most practitioners tend to favor entity buy-out agreements whereby the *put* is to the corporation, and likewise the corporation has the option to buy if the put is not exercised. This is particularly convenient, apart from the tax laws, when more than three shareholders are involved in a corporation. The difficulty with multiple shareholders is that you may get into an endless round of offers and participants when one of the shareholders does not take up his pro rata share of the initial offer. The same thing happens in the second go-around, etc.

RESTRICTIONS ON TRANSFER OF STOCK

During the course of the buy-sell agreement, the stock certificates should bear a legend stating that they are subject to a buy-sell agreement. Otherwise, a bona fide purchaser for value, without notice of the stock legend, would cut off the rights of the other parties under the buy-sell agreement. Provision should be made to determine whether the shareholder can use the stock as collateral and whether he must have the consent of the other parties to do so. Attention should be given to the question of whether the shareholder can transfer stock to other family members as if it were actually owned by the shareholder, so long as it remains subject to the buy-sell agreement, which is triggered by the same events regarding the shareholder. This will facilitate estate planning within the group, and is usually a good idea.

7

Dealing with Business Brokers

Businessmen who decide to buy a business or expand their existing business by acquisitions will inevitably encounter the business broker. Lots of people get into trouble by blindly accepting the services of these gentlemen. Remember that the broker's interest is in earning a commission, not in crossing the *t*s and dotting the *i*s in terms of his relationship with the parties.

If you decide you need the help of a broker, be sure you have an agreement with him. The first rule here is not to sign the agreement he presents to you. It will be open-ended and continue for a longer period of time that you want it to continue; it may well be exclusive, preventing you from dealing with other brokers who bring you opportunities, and perhaps preventing you from proceeding independently. His agreement will define a "commissionable sale" in very broad terms, such as, *introduction of the buyer and the seller, or the final consummation of a transaction.* These things may occur whether or not the broker performs any real services. It is important to limit commissionable transactions to those that are actually closed, and to those in which the broker played a significant role beyond that of simply identifying or introducing the parties. A broker occasionally takes advantage of broad provisions by filing a whole list of possible candidates with the prospective buyer, and later claiming to be the introducing broker even though he had nothing further to do with the transaction. Limit the broker's representation to a nonexclusive basis for a sixty- or a ninety-day period, or some similarly reasonable time. It is possible to provide that in the event he performs services in conjunction with a transaction initiated by another broker, he will share in that commission, but to exclude the possibility of other transactions for a long period of time is unwise. Likewise, it is well to exclude from the agreement identified companies with which you are already familiar or have a contact. There is no sense in paying a commission on a deal where you end up buying Uncle Harry's business. Unless you are careful, it could happen.

In case a dispute arises between you and the broker over his commission, it might be worthwhile to check to see if he is properly licensed in the state in which you are located or in which the transaction took place. Some states require business brokers to hold a real estate agent's license. Other states require a securities broker's license. Out-of-state brokers are often not aware of these local requirements. We have seen cases where a broker's commission was successfully denied him by the establishment of his failure to have the proper license in the state in question. Most such statutes prohibit the collection of a commission if the broker is not properly licensed. Other licensing laws can be found under the securities law of the particular state, or in some cases, under a business broker's law. Typically, a phone call to one of those state agencies will provide you with the initial information about licensing requirements and about whether your particular individual is properly licensed.

Do not let a broker wander the field in an uncontrolled

manner, telling everyone that he represents you in negotiations. Know who he is going to talk to, and know what he is going to say. Insist on regular and periodic reports. Otherwise, you may find yourself committed to liability producing situations.

One area of difficulty with brokers is in the realm of confidential and proprietary information. If your broker relates to you information that has been disclosed to him about a target company's market, its new product plans, or a particular manufacturing process which is not generally known to the public, you may well be found liable for misuse of such proprietary or confidential information. This can happen even if you thereafter innocently create the process yourself, or independently develop it in your own business. Your burden of proof will be extremely heavy once it is shown that you had previously received confidential information. In other words, your later ability to compete in that field will be seriously restricted by your receipt of confidential or proprietary information in connection with the investigation of the target company. Furthermore, the likelihood of a lawsuit under those circumstances is very high, inasmuch as the target company may well have a bad taste in its mouth following the termination of negotiations, and so be delighted to have found a reason to bring a lawsuit when it thinks you have misused its business secrets. Remember, "Hell hath no fury like that of a target scorned."

Be sure you know what kind of relationship your broker may have had in the past with the target company or others involved in the transaction. The broker who has previously received information about a target because he was the target's agent, or who has information from a confidential source, may be stopped from using it, and your transaction may be stopped through his use of that information in a conflict of interest situation. A good broker will always make a disclosure of this kind of thing, but it does not hurt to inquire.

Feel free to insist that your broker provide real services throughout the transaction, not just at the introductory stage.

There are certain difficult points in a negotiation which a broker, as a third party, can assist in resolving. If he stays close to the negotiations without interfering until he is asked to do so, he can provide these good offices after everyone stalks out of the room in a fit of anger over some dispute. The broker's quiet persuasiveness can find a way to bridge the gap. However, if he is off in Timbuktu working on another deal, he is not going to be much good to you. Make him earn his commission. This includes the process of drafting and closing as well. Inevitably, closings of significant transactions produce difficulties in the last few days. I have never seen a so-called "pro forma" closing where the papers are shuffled by the lawyers, in that glorious old phrase, and everything is done by ten o'clock in the morning. Little things that people have left until the end have a way of coming up at that point because they are painful or uncomfortable or were simply overlooked. Be prepared to do some work at the bitter end, and be prepared to have your broker there to help out if needed. However, in the end, do not expect your broker to make a deal for you. Deals are made by principals, seldom by intermediaries. The two principals will have to have a meeting of the minds on the substantial issues and will then have to stay involved to make sure that small details do not run the transaction off the rails.

8

Warranties

EXPRESS AND IMPLIED WARRANTIES

This section offers an overview of warranty law.

The Uniform Commercial Code (which governs sales transactions and other matters, and has been adopted by nearly every state) recognizes express warranties and two kinds of implied warranties: merchantability, and fitness for the particular purpose. Express warranties are easy to recognize in their normal form, but the courts have found some unusual forms as well. Implied warranties arise by operation of law and commercial dealing. Express warranties have to be made by someone. The courts have recognized a large number of agents who can make express warranties binding on their principal.

Authority to Make Express Warranties

The normal sales transaction involves sale of goods by a

manufacturer to a distributor to a dealer to a consumer. Can the consumer sue the manufacturer for statements made by the salesperson that constitute express warranties? If the salesperson was an agent of the manufacturer, the manufacturer is liable for the express warranty. In the absence of actual authority from the manufacturer to make such warranties, the courts have frequently found implied or apparent authority. In some cases, liability has been found even though the principal had instructed the salesperson not to warrant the goods. The Restatement of Agency, Section 63(1) provides,

> Unless otherwise agreed, the authority to sell includes authority to make such promises operating as warranties and only such as are usual in such a transaction.

Liability of dealers for express warranties made by manufacturers has produced some confusion in the courts. It has been held in some cases that the warranty must be adopted by the dealer in order to make the dealer liable. In most situations, however, the courts have found that unless the dealer was without knowledge of the manufacturer's warranty, he was obliged to fulfill it.

Typically, the manufacturer's warranty card contains a disclaimer of authority on the part of any dealer or salesperson to make any warranties other than those stated on the card. Is a consumer bound by that limitation? In many cases, such as a toaster or other appliance, the warranty material is packed in the box that the consumer opens at home after the purchase. Likely, it does not get read even then. The effectiveness of such a limitation is highly questionable.

Notice of Breach of Warranty

A common law notice of breach of warranty to the seller is not necessarily prerequisite to a suit based on the breach. The code quite clearly requires notice with respect to commercial loss but probably not with respect to consumer losses, particularly losses for personal injury or property damage.

Implied Warranty of Merchantability

Just what "merchantable" means has always been an elusive matter. It seems to be a concept lurking just beyond one's final grasp, although at times it rolls off the tongue with a degree of confidence born only of faith. The best example given in the Uniform Commercial Code says that goods must be fit for the ordinary purposes for which such goods are used. It suggests that food, for example, must be fit for human consumption. Cosmetics, for example, must be fit for use upon the skin. It might also mean that a dealer who buys goods from a manufacturer for resale is entitled to expect that those goods are honestly resalable in the ordinary course. Another concept is that the goods must pass without objection in the trade, or otherwise meet normal commercial standards.

Note that this warranty arises only when the seller is a merchant with respect to the goods at the time sold. An isolated sale of your used car would not carry an implied warranty of merchantability. Unhappily, however, if there is a hidden defect known to the seller but not discoverable by inspection, the obligation of good faith may be breached and liability imposed upon the seller, even in such isolated sales. If, however, there were no evidence that the seller knew, or ought to have known, that the funny noise underneath the floorboards was a defective ring gear, then there would be no liability.

Implied Warranty of Fitness for a Particular Purpose

Section 2-315 of the Uniform Commercial Code provides,

> Where the seller at the time of contracting has reason to know any particular purpose for which the goods are required and that the buyer is relying on the seller's skill or judgment to select or furnish suitable goods, there is, unless excluded or modified under the next section, an implied warranty that the goods shall be fit for such purpose.

In this section, an element of reliance that is not present in other warranty sections is required. This is reliance upon the seller's skill or judgment in selecting or furnishing suitable goods. This warranty applies to merchants as well as nonmerchants. An illustration of the distinction between merchantability and fitness warranties is found in a New York case in which Judge Cardozo held that there was no warranty of fitness where one purchases a specified article under its patent or other trade name. The plaintiff bought a loaf of Wards Bread at a local grocery store. The bread proved to have a nail in it, causing injury. The New York Court of Appeals held that there was no warranty of fitness for a particular purpose because the bread was purchased by a trade name and the plaintiff chose it herself. Consequently, there was no reliance on the skill of the seller. On the other hand, the court did find there was a breach of implied warranty of merchantability.

In many cases, both warranties will arise at the same time. On the other hand, they may not. Furthermore, in any given case, there can be a breach of one and not of the other. The warranty of merchantability applies only to the ordinary purpose for which the goods are made and are to be used and not to the specialty of the buyer. If, however, the buyer makes known his needs to the seller or the seller knows of the particular purpose and selects the goods, such selection may be relied upon by the buyer. There would then be a breach of warranty of fitness for the particular purpose. Shoes are generally used for walking, but the seller may know that a particular pair was selected or required for use in mountain climbing.

PERSONAL INJURY

Strict Liability

The manufacturer can be liable to an injured user. Section 402A of the Restatement, Torts covers this question. The manufacturer can do very little in drafting his warranty language or designing his marketing techniques to protect himself against liability for personal injury in jurisdictions that have adopted strict liability in tort. However, the fact that the doctrine of strict liability has been substantially adopted in this country does not eliminate the need for concern about liability on a warranty theory. There remain a certain number of states where strict liability is not yet the law, and disclaimers can be helpful in such jurisdictions. Most strict liability cases will also be tried on negligence and warranty theories.

The Code—Limitation of Remedy

With regard to damages for personal injuries, the Uniform Commercial Code provides in Section 2-719 that *consequential damages* may be limited or excluded unless the limitation or exclusion is unconscionable. Limitation of consequential damages for injury to the person in the case of consumer goods is prima facie unconscionable, but limitation of damages when the loss is commercial is not.

In an Arkansas case, the accident victim had purchased a pickup truck from a Ford dealer. The dealer was sued on an implied warranty of fitness. The dealer filed a third-party claim against Ford. The Arkansas Supreme Court held that the truck was consumer goods, and the dealer's disclaimers of liability for personal injuries and limitation of remedies were unconscionable. As between the dealer and Ford, Ford claimed that its identical limitation and disclaimer was not unconscionable because the truck was inventory in the hands of the dealer. The court rejected this argument and went on to say that "nothing could be more unconscionable than to hold the dealer, a mere conduit between the manufacturer and the ultimate consumer, liable for consequential damages, on the breach of an implied warranty for fault or defect caused by the automobile manufacturer of which the dealer had no notice or knowledge." In commercial damage cases, by contrast, the courts have given effect to limitations of liability for consequential damages.

In summary, a manufacturer is interested in an appropriate disclaimer or warranty limitation and in the nature of its express warranties because (a) even in personal injury cases the plaintiff will be relying in part on a warranty theory; (b) there are certain states which have not adopted the doctrine of strict liability; (c) liability for repair, return, replacement, or damages of a commercial nature can be limited.

9

What to Do about Defective Goods, Machinery, and Equipment

UNWARRANTIED *VERSUS* WARRANTIED

If you are unfortunate enough to have purchased defective goods, machinery, or equipment, the first question you should ask yourself is whether or not what you purchased has a warranty. The next question to ask is whether the warranty is written or implied as a matter of law. Frequently, buyers overlook the possibility that there may be implied warranties protecting them. Finally, if the warranty is written, the question should be asked whether it is written in a way that actually adds to your rights, or so narrowly that it restricts or limits them.

A further word on warranties: a writing or statement need not be labeled "warranty" or "guaranty" to be a warranty. The Uniform Commercial Code provides that *any affirmation of fact* can be a warranty, whether or not it is designed as such. Thus, statements made in advertising, brochures, letters, contracts, or other documents can be written warranties, and statements made verbally to you can be oral warranties. Indeed, with the sophistication of modern lawyers, you may be better off having a good written statement of some sort—which was never intended to be a warranty—than a narrowly drafted "warranty," which lawyers are always drafting for their clients in order to severely limit the extent to which they have to stand behind their goods, machinery, and equipment. One lesson is obvious here: save everything (particularly advertising and other materials) which you receive in the course of buying goods, machinery, or equipment. Such materials may include warranties the seller never dreamed he was making!

UNWRITTEN WARRANTIES AVAILABLE AS A MATTER OF LAW

Warranties which arise as a matter of law are called "implied warranties." The two most common are the implied warranty of merchantability and the implied warranty of fitness for the use intended. These are warranties that are available on nearly all goods, equipment, and machinery under the Uniform Commercial Code and under the law of most states. Many states have modified these implied warranties somewhat by construing them differently in various cases. Nevertheless, in most instances, if you purchase goods from a manufacturer, there is an implied warranty that they are of merchantable quality. If you purchase machinery or equipment for a specific use, there is an implied warranty that it is fit for the use intended. Obviously, reasonable men can differ about what is merchantable or fit for an intended use. However, unless you have made an agreement to the contrary, these are warranties that you can rely upon regardless of whether they have been written down.

LIMITATIONS, EXCLUSIONS, OR MODIFICATIONS OF WARRANTIES

Under the Uniform Commercial Code, in order to exclude

or modify the implied warranty of merchantability, language must expressly mention merchantability and it must be conspicuous. The same goes for the warranty of fitness. In addition, implied warranties can be eradicated by the insertion of words in a contract or receipt, etc., such as "as is" or "with all faults," if, under normal circumstances, everyone understands the meaning of this language. In addition, if the buyer, before entering into a contract to purchase, has examined the goods or a sample or model as fully as he feels is necessary, or if he has refused to make an examination that was offered, there is no implied warranty with regard to defects that his examination revealed or that any reasonable examination would have revealed. In addition, in the normal course of performance or usage, implied warranties can be excluded or modified, by a course of dealing, or of a trade or industry.

A general legal principle involved in this area of the law is that *any written disclaimer or limitation of warranty is strictly construed against the seller.* Since the seller is better able to hire a lawyer to carefully draft a clause, the clause will be construed as strongly as possible against the one who drafts it. In addition, it is a general policy to permit parties to a contract to modify warranties but to protect the buyer against any exclusions, modifications, or limitations of warranties that he did not bargain for. For this reason, any such language must be clear and unambiguous, and must put the buyer on fair notice. Further, the buyer must fully agree with those terms, and the disclaimer of warranties must be part of the basis for the bargain.

In addition, there are many statutes which protect consumers, farmers, and other specified classes of buyers from any disclaimers of warranties. Statutes should be checked to determine whether they protect you if you run up against a limitation of a warranty. For example, in North Dakota, there is a statute that provides that if tractors are not reasonably fit for the purpose for which they are purchased, the buyer can rescind the deal, and any disclaimer of the implied warranty of fitness for use is void. In Wisconsin, the State Motor Vehicle Act provides that a seller cannot disclaim the warranty of title that he makes when he sells a car.

Further, in most states, if there is public policy involved, such as safety standards, a disclaimer of warranty will not negate a manufacturer's liability for negligently manufacturing dangerous goods.

In addition, disclaimers of merchantability and fitness for use must be in conspicuous places, not hidden in the fine print of a delivery ticket, purchase order, or other document. Various factors have been applied by the courts in determining whether or not a disclaimer is conspicuous, such as whether it is set in bold type, or in type of different color, or face, or whether it is underscored, legible, etc. This goes for words such as "as is" and for more elaborately drafted disclaimers of warranties.

The following is an example of a clause that is probably a pretty good disclaimer of implied warranties, except for those on consumer goods.

IMPORTANT NOTICE

SELLER MAKES <u>NO WARRANTIES</u>, EXPRESS OR IM-PLIED, INCLUDING THE IMPLIED WARRANTIES OF <u>MERCHANTABILITY</u> AND <u>FITNESS FOR A PARTICULAR PURPOSE</u> REGARDING ANY AND ALL GOODS, MER-CHANDISE, OR EQUIPMENT SOLD UNDER THIS CON-TRACT, AND IT IS HEREBY AGREED BY BOTH PARTIES THAT THE BUYER PURCHASES THESE GOODS, MA-CHINERY, OR EQUIPMENT <u>AS IS</u> AND <u>WITH ALL OF THEIR FAULTS</u>. The foregoing contract is the complete, final, and exclusive agreement of the parties, and both parties affirm that they have not relied on any statements by the seller or buyer of their agents not expressly stated in this contract, and that any such statements are not part of the basis for this contract.

If you want to limit warranties in any goods, machinery, or equipment you sell, and there is no state law (either statutory or case law) that prevents it, you ought to use strong language of the nature set forth in the example. A word of caution here: the example is not intended to be copied and included in contracts by purchasers of this book without checking with their own lawyers in their own states. Exclusion and limitation of warranties is a tricky area of the law, and the authors do not recommend attempting to embark upon it without legal advice tailored to each individual's circumstances.

UNCONSCIONABILITY

In addition to the foregoing principles which apply to exclusions of warranties and other clauses in contracts, there is a common law doctrine called "unconscionability." Defined in an old English case and followed by the United States Supreme Court, unconscionability is an agreement "such as no man in his senses and not under delusion would make on the one hand, and as no honest and fair man would accept on the other." Some limitations and exclusions of warranties are so clearly unfair that the courts simply will not enforce them. There are other related common law doctrines which stop parties from enforcing unfair contracts, such as misrepresentation and fraud, duress, and undue influence. Factors which are considered by the courts in determining whether a contract or other arrangement is unconscionable are any kind of unfair dealing or overreaching by one party, taking into account whether one party or the other has a lack of understanding or an ignorance of the fact, whether there is grossly unequal bargaining power, whether there is no choice on the part of the party who accepts a deal, whether there is an inability to understand the English language or fine print or tricky legal terms, whether the industry generally regards certain things as fair or unfair, whether high pressure sales tactics were used, and various statutes which protect specific classes of buyers, such as farmers, consumers, etc. Once again, a search for such defenses against an assertion of a limitation of warranty depends greatly upon the law of the particular state involved.

REFUSAL OF ACCEPTANCE

If a buyer purchases defective goods, he has a right to refuse to accept goods within a reasonable time or, if he has accepted the goods but has not inspected them quickly enough, he has a right to revoke his acceptance of the goods—if he has sufficient justification. Generally, the buyer has a right to reject any goods which fail to conform to the contract under which he bought them. However, once the buyer rejects, the seller has a right to cure the defect. Please take note that we are talking here about goods that are bought in the course of business.

In addition, sometimes it is not commercially feasible for the buyer to reject the goods because he needs them, even though they are defective. If this is the case, the buyer has the right to accept the goods (if he gives the seller reasonable notice) and to use them and seek damages from the seller. Again, however, the seller, upon receipt of proper notification, has the right to cure the defect.

In situations where the buyer has rejected the goods or where he has justifiably revoked his acceptance of the goods, the buyer has remedies, which include cancellation of the contract, recovery of the price paid, or a security interest in goods that he keeps in his possession or control if the seller does not refund his money, which he can enforce by selling the goods and going after the seller for recovery of damages.

In a situation where the buyer has finally accepted the goods, he has a right to sue for damages. These damages are generally measured by the difference between the value of the goods accepted and the value they would have had if at the time and place of acceptance, they had been in the condition agreed upon in the contract. In addition, in certain cases the buyer can recover incidental damages occasioned by the seller's breach of contract, and, in some instances, consequential damages. These damages include any loss resulting from the buyer's general or particular requirements or needs, which the seller, at the time of contracting, had reason to know about.

Such consequential damages sometimes include the loss of profits. Once again, if damages from defective goods purchased by your business are substantial, you should have a thorough analysis of your rights made by your lawyer.

EVIDENCE

As stated throughout this book, the key to prevailing in many cases involving breach of contracts of all sorts, including defective goods, equipment, or machinery, is preservation of evidence. Documentation, photographing, witness statements, affidavits—all of the means of preserving evidence mentioned elsewhere in this book apply to this section. This goes particularly for the notification of defectiveness which must be given to the seller. Such notices, if at all possible, should be sent by certified or registered mail and copies should be retained. Once equipment, machinery, or goods are discovered to be defective, all advertising and other materials should be rounded up as soon as possible and put in a safe place. Inspections by third party experts should be made, and the reports should be obtained from them and then be forwarded to the seller, particularly in the case of large and expensive items of machinery and equipment. Payments which are due under equipment leases, and things of this nature, should be put in escrow or withheld with proper precautions (once again, confirmed by consultation with your lawyer). Upon discovery of defects in goods, machinery, or equipment, it is time, euphemistically, to "cover your posterior." The best way to do this is with plenty of correspondence setting forth the circumstances and putting the seller on notice of your complaints. Do this both initially and as the seller seeks to excuse his nonperformance or cure the defects.

Do not forget damages. If you are suffering consequential damages in the form of lost business, profits, etc., because of defective goods, machinery, or equipment, do everything you can to create and preserve evidence of such losses. Such action will probably prove invaluable in the event you have to go to court to enforce your rights.

REQUIREMENTS TO RETURN TO A PARTICULAR PLACE FOR REPAIR

In a contract, an inserted clause stating that the seller has no obligation to repair a product unless it is returned to his plant in rural Afghanistan, freight prepaid, packaged in velvet, is clearly too unreasonable to be enforced. Never acquiesce in a return for repair clause without questioning it, and probably never without a fight, unless you expressly bargained for such a deal.

10

Termination of Employment: Protecting Your Business from Raids by Departing Employees

CONTRACTUAL PROTECTION—NONCOMPETITION AGREEMENTS

Probably no contractual provisions generate more activity in the courts than noncompetition clauses in employment agreements. Because of this, controversy has arisen as to whether it is a good idea to include them in agreements at all. Many judges and some state supreme courts do not like them and go to great pains to find them invalid. In nearly all jurisdictions in the United States, however, a reasonably drafted noncompetition agreement is enforceable. In some states, there are statutes which either curtail their use or make them illegal. For this reason, if you wish to include one in an employment agreement, it is advisable to consult your lawyer to determine whether or not statutory limitations exist. If they do not, serious consideration should be given to the reasoning behind including a noncompetition agreement in a contract.

Arguments have been made against noncompetition agreements on the grounds that they seem to always generate lawsuits and that if you treat your employees fairly in the first place, they are unnecessary. It has been the experience of the authors that reasonably drafted noncompetition agreements are enforceable. There are certain industries where piracy seems to be the watchword. Further, there are certain employees who cannot be trusted no matter how well they are treated. In such cases, a written noncompetition agreement can be invaluable in protecting your business. Rather than going to court armed with nothing other than the rather loose, common law prohibitions against unfair competition, it is much better to be in possession of a well drafted, signed document establishing what behavior both parties agree is unfair competition and acknowledging the damages that would flow from such unfair competition.

You will note that we use the word "reasonable" in describing a helpful noncompetition clause. In general, the courts will enforce a noncompetition clause only to the extent to which it is reasonable, both in the territory covered by the clause and the amount of time during which competition is prohibited. There seems to be a constant battle between the drafting attorney and the client in this regard; the client wants to take in as much territory and time as possible, whereas the careful draftsman, having read the case law on enforcement of noncompetition clauses, knows that the courts will consistently refuse to enforce a noncompetition clause which overreaches, either in time or territory.

A recent trend has somewhat alleviated this conflict. That is, rather than throwing out entire noncompetition agreements if they tend to be overreaching, the more modern tendency of the courts has been to pare the time and territory down to what the court deems "reasonable." Nevertheless, it is still a very bad idea to bring into court a clause which is clearly overreaching. If you do business in only one state, don't try to enforce a noncompetition clause covering the entire nation. Have the noncompetition clause cover only the territory where you need protection. Further, if it takes only six months to train a new man to be as competitive as a departing employee was, don't attempt a clause that enjoins a departing employee from competing for thirty-six months. Even if the court would reform such an agreement to cover only one state and for only six months after termination of employment, it does you no good to have the trial judge from whom you are requesting relief believe that you are an overreaching, punitive sort of employer. You may also be asking the judge for money damages, which will undoubtedly be awarded at his discretion. If the court does not like you, you can guess what kind of damages you are likely to get.

Plenty of thought should be given to whether you need to include all your employees. In a famous Minnesota case, Standard Oil had a noncompetition agreement with a service station employee. The court refused to enforce it, pointing out that a court of equity simply was not going to regard the amount of damage a little gas pump jockey could inflict upon Standard Oil as significant, balancing the relative hardship of the parties to the lawsuit. Don't let this be your mistake; only use noncompetition agreements to protect you from the competition of a former employee who can actually hurt you. On the other hand, it is good to be uniform throughout your business. If you have a staff of fifty salesmen and ask only five of them to sign an agreement, you can be sure that the one of the five who quits to compete with you will claim discrimination and point to the fact that the other forty-five did not have to sign such agreements.

The type of relief set forth in noncompetition agreements is generally twofold: injunctive relief, preventing the employee by court order from doing something; and money relief, or damages, to compensate for the harm the employee creates by competing. It is important in such clauses to spell out the fact that both types of relief will be granted.

Injunctive Relief

An injunction is a court order, or writ, specifically stopping someone from doing something or forcing someone to do something. Most noncompetition injunction clauses specifically point out to the employee that injunctive relief can be obtained by application to a court of competent jurisdiction if the employee violates the clause. A jury trial cannot be obtained in an injunction case, since it is "equitable" relief. Therefore, judges nearly always decide noncompetition clause issues. This is probably favorable to the employer, because juries have a way of sympathizing with the underdog.

Damages, or Money Relief

The authors recommend that the type of money relief to be awarded in the event of breach of a noncompetition clause be spelled out. Once again, the watchword ought to be restraint in drafting such a clause, taking care not to overreach. If a clause that calls for damages in a specified sum is realistic, it can be awarded as *liquidated damages*. If it is simply a clause designed to frighten the employee into remaining in the employ of the employer (an *in terrorem clause*) it will in all likelihood be unenforceable in court. Much case law is devoted to determining if clauses are truly liquidated damages or are *"in terrorem."*

One way of mitigating the appearance of overreaching is to avoid using a set sum in your damages clause and to employ a formula (sometimes called "average daily damage"), based on the amount of time the employee continues to violate the clause, to determine the amount of money awarded. Such formulas call for taking into account the gross amount of business the employee averaged over a realistic period, such as the last six months of his employment, dividing by the number of days, and then figuring out the daily net profit the employer would typically make on such a gross and multiply it by the number of days the ex-employee operates in competition with the employer.

Basic damages clauses, utilizing set sums and those that utilize a formula, in the opinion of the authors, can have a marked effect upon ex-employees. The reasoning is simple: if there are no damage clauses, it is easy for a lawyer to advise the employee that he has little to lose by going to work for a competitor. All he risks is the possibility of being enjoined and having to work elsewhere for a while. If there is a possibility of considerable damages, however, regardless of how remote the possibility that the former employer will win them, the lawyer to whom the employee has gone for advice will be very hard put to advise him that he has nothing to fear. This may well stop an employee from competing who otherwise would be tempted. The employer may never know how beneficial such a noncompetition damages clause was!

Here are two noncompetition sections from employment agreements, one with an "average daily damage" formula and one with a straight, money damage formula.

AGREEMENT WITH STRAIGHT MONEY DAMAGES

Noncompetition Agreement. It is understood and agreed that Employee, in the course of his activities on behalf of Corporation, will be placed in a close, personal, and confidential relationship with existing clients of Corporation and will be forming such relationships with new clients in the course of his activities on behalf of Corporation. It is further understood and agreed that in light of the foregoing relationship with Corporation's clients, Corporation will be irreparably damaged in the event Employee terminates his employment with Corporation and commences business or accepts an employment position with another competing corporation within Camelot County within a period of two (2) years after his termination with Corporation. Consequently, Employee agrees that he will not commence competitive employment within Camelot County for a period of two (2) years after his termination of employment with Corporation, nor will he accept employment in any form from any competing corporation located within Camelot County for a period of two (2) years after the termination of his employment with Corporation.

Injunctive Relief. It being recognized by both Corporation and Employee that irreparable damage will result to Corporation if Employee violates the foregoing paragraph hereof, it is hereby agreed that in the event of any breach of any of said paragraph by Employee or apparent danger of such breach, Corporation shall be entitled, in addition to all remedies available to it, to an injunction to restrain the violation of any of the covenants of said paragraph by Employee.

Liquidated Damages. It is recognized by both Corporation and Employee that actual damages resulting from a breach of the foregoing paragraph *(Noncompetition Agreement)* hereof by Employee will be very difficult or impossible to ascertain and that Employee, in the event he violates said paragraph, will be employing and utilizing valuable training, experience with Corporation's clients and client contact provided him by Corporation; therefore, in the event of any breach of the covenants of said paragraph, Employee agrees to pay to Corporation, as liquidated damages in satisfaction of the claims of Corporation for any such breach and as payment for such training, experience, and valuable client contacts, the sum of Fifty Thousand Dollars ($50,000) liquidated damages. It is agreed that this provision for liquidated damages is fair and equitable and that the amount set forth is reasonable under the circumstances.

Nonwaiver, Separability, Applicable Law, and Successorship. The failure of Corporation at any time to insist upon strict adherence to any one or more of the covenants and restrictions herein shall not be construed as a waiver of the rights of Corporation to require their strict compliance thereafter or to any other covenant or restriction therein. The provisions of this agreement are intended to be separate, and where the context permits, portions of a particular provision are intended to be separate from all other portions of that provision. In the event a particular provision or provisions or any portion thereof, are determined to be invalid or unenforceable, it is intended and agreed, nevertheless, that the remaining provisions of this agreement shall continue to be valid and enforceable in all respects. This agreement shall be construed pursuant to the laws of the State of Minnesota. This agreement shall be binding upon and inure to the benefit of Corporation, its successors, and assigns.

AGREEMENT WITH DAILY DAMAGE FORMULA

THIS AGREEMENT, made _____ , 19 ____ , by and between *Earnest Employment Agency Inc.*, hereinafter referred to as the "Company" and *Danny Disloyal* , hereinafter referred to as the "Employee."

WITNESSETH:

WHEREAS, the Company has developed valuable relationships with both applicants and employers, which enable the Company to produce sufficient income to compensate its employees; and

WHEREAS, the Company has developed valuable confidential techniques and valuable proprietary and confidential forms and methods; and

WHEREAS, the *employee* desires to learn said valuable techniques and employ said valuable forms and methods in earning income as an *agent* in the employ of the Company; and

WHEREAS, the *employee* acknowledges that he does not presently possess sufficient knowledge of the techniques, forms, and methods of the Company to proficiently operate as an ___*agent*___ in the manner contemplated by both himself and the Company; and

WHEREAS, both parties hereto acknowledge that the position of ___*agent*___ is one of considerable responsibility and requiring such considerable training, relationships, and contacts with employers and experience that it will take the Company, under favorable circumstances, at least twelve months to replace an ___*agent*___ who has received such training, relationships, and contacts with employers and experiences as are typically afforded by the Company,

NOW, THEREFORE, in consideration of the premises and the mutual covenants of the parties herein set forth, it is hereby agreed:

1. That the Company hereby employs *Danny Disloyal* as an ___*agent*___ , in which capacity the ___*employee*___ agrees to expend his full time and best efforts toward obtaining employment positions for applicants and employees for employers to whom the Company has agreed to furnish such services.

2. That the Company agrees to assume all usual and ordinary expenses involved in furnishing the ___*employee*___ with appropriate offices and working conditions.

3. That the Company agrees to furnish the ___*employee*___ with its confidential and proprietary techniques, forms, and methods for the ___*employee's*___ use in his employment by the Company.

4. That the ___*employee*___ shall conduct his business in accordance with the directives of the Company and in such a manner as to maintain and increase the goodwill and the reputation of the Company.

5. That the *employee* shall not have authority to make any type of contract or agreement on behalf of the Company or otherwise subject the Company to any claim or liability except the normal arrangements made in the *employee's* obtaining of employment positions for applicants and employees for employers or as otherwise directed by the Company.

6. That as compensation for services to be rendered by the *employee*, the Company agrees . . . (terms of pay).

7. That the techniques, forms, methods, records, and materials employed by or obtained by the *employee* in the course of his employment with the Company are confidential and shall remain the exclusive property and proprietary information of the Company. The *employee* agrees that during the term of this agreement he will not deliver such techniques, forms, methods, records, or materials to any person, nor will he, at any time after termination of his employment hereunder, utilize such techniques, forms, methods, records, or materials for any purpose whatsoever, without the express written consent of the Company.

8. That it is understood and agreed that the *employee*, in the course of his activities on behalf of the Company, will receive and have access to certain confidential, proprietary information constituting the trade secrets of the Company, including but not limited to the identity of applicants for employment positions, the personal information supplied by applicants for employment, information concerning and the identity of employers and personnel in the employ of employers and the terms and conditions in the same business, its branches and affiliates, as well as its suppliers and contacts. The *employee* hereby agrees that he will not make use of any such information, nor disclose it to any other person, firm, corporation, or association, without the express written

consent of the Company, either during the term of this agreement or at any time after its termination.

9. That recognizing the potential damage to the Company in the event the *employee* violates the provisions of paragraphs 1, 3, 4, 7, or 8 hereof, it is agreed that the *employee* shall not, for a period of one year after the termination of this agreement with the Company, regardless of whether such termination is voluntary or involuntary, engage directly or indirectly, either personally or as an employee, associate, partner, manager, owner, agent, or otherwise, in the same business as that of the Company or any successor to the Company's business, or contact any applicant or employer in the course of such business, within the counties of Camelot and _____ *Oz* _____ in the State of *Minnesota* in any manner which involves any applicant with whom the *employee* had contact or access to during the last year of his employ by the Company, or involving any employer with whom the *employee* had contact or access to during the last year of employ by the Company. The parties hereto acknowledge that the one year term, the territory of Camelot and _____ *Oz* _____ counties, and the limitation to accounts and companies dealt with by the *employee* during the last year of the *employee's* employ are the minimum protections necessary to safeguard the Company's business until the Company is able to train and develop a suitable replacement _____ *agent* _____ .

10. That if the *employee* , within one year subsequent to termination of this agreement, accepts an employment position with another employer as the direct or indirect result of information possessed by the Company, it is agreed that the *employee* will pay the Company the normal placement fee for such employment position in accordance with the Company's then current placement fee schedule.

11. That the *employee* agrees to pay over to the Company any commission, compensation, gratuity, or other emolument of any kind received during the term of this agreement from any employer or applicant in connection with the placement of any person for employment, regardless of whether such placement falls within the scope of the *employee's* ordinary business activities and regardless of whether such placement should occur.

12. That upon termination of this agreement for any reason, the *employee* shall immediately turn over to the Company any and all lists, documents, or other types of records, and any written, typed, or printed materials identifying the applicants of the Company or identifying the employers or personnel of employers, together with any and all data involving advertising techniques, applicant processing, forms, correspondence, or data in any way involving the Company's techniques, training manuals, materials, programs, methods, or contacts, and that the *employee* shall have no right to retain any copies of the foregoing for any reason whatsoever after termination of his employment by the Company without the express written consent of the Company.

13. Recognizing that irreparable damage will result to the Company if the *employee* violates paragraphs 7, 8, 9, or 12 hereof, it is hereby agreed that in the event of any breach of said paragraphs by the *employee* or apparent danger of such breach, the Company shall be entitled, in addition to such other remedies available to it, to an injunction to restrain the violation of any or all such covenants by the *employee* .

14. Recognizing that actual damages resulting from breach of paragraph 9 hereof by the *employee* will be difficult or impossible to ascertain and that the *employee* , by such violation, will be employing the valuable training and

experience afforded him by the Company; therefore, in the event of such breach, the *employee* agrees to pay to the Company as liquidated damages in satisfaction of the claims of the Company for such breach and as payment for such training and experience, the following:

a. $2,500, plus

b. "Average daily damage," or the total amount of gross profit, less compensation payable to the *employee* , as defined in paragraph 6 of this agreement, earned by the Company on placements made by the *employee* during the one-year period immediately preceding the date of termination of this agreement, or the full period of this agreement if it is not in force for more than one year, divided by the number of business days in such period (a "business day" is any day except Saturday, Sunday, or legal holiday), multiplied by the number of days in which the *employee* engages in activities constituting a breach of paragraph 9 hereof.

It is agreed that this provision for liquidated damages is fair and equitable and that the amounts set forth above are reasonable under the circumstances.

15. That the failure of the Company to insist upon strict adherence to one or more of the covenants and restrictions herein shall not be construed as a waiver of the rights of the Company to require strict compliance thereafter or to any other covenant or restriction herein.

16. That the provisions of this agreement are intended to be separate and, where the context permits, portions of a particular provision are intended to be separate from all other portions of that provision. In the event that a particular provision or provisions, or any portion thereof, are determined

to be invalid or unenforceable, it is intended and agreed, nevertheless, that the remaining provisions of this agreement shall continue to be valid and enforceable in all respects.

17. That this agreement shall be construed pursuant to the laws of the State of _Minnesota_ .

18. That this agreement shall be binding upon and inure to the benefit of the Company, its successors, and assigns.

19. That the _employee's_ interests hereunder are not assignable.

IN WITNESS WHEREOF, the parties have executed this agreement the date and year first above written.

UNFAIR COMPETITION CASES

While reading the foregoing portion of this section, you may be asking yourself "What can I do if I do not have a specific agreement protecting me?" Many employers simply are not in a position to get their employees to sign a noncompetition agreement; and yet, they are susceptible to piracy of their trade secrets and business by disloyal ex-employees. If the behavior of the ex-employee is sufficiently egregious, there is a possibility of a lawsuit for unfair competition.

There are some basic legal principles which assist the employer here: as long as an employee is receiving a paycheck and is in your employ, he owes you a *duty of loyalty*. Consequently, if it can be established that the employee, while still in your employ, was running the photocopy machine overtime or otherwise availing himself of information that is proprietary, such as trade secrets in the manufacturing process, the identities and preferences of customers, pricing information, and other data, you have some powerful facts on your side. If you can prove he removed the information from your business premises and did not return it, in all likelihood you can get the information returned and you have a good chance at getting a damages award if he has used the information to your detriment.

In order to shore up the strength of such a case, there are things you can do before any employee leaves. Your company should have a uniform policy of instructing all employees, preferably in writing to serve as evidence later, that certain information is proprietary and confidential and is not to be taken out of the business premises, disseminated, or used by persons not in your employ. Strangers should be kept out of production areas where trade secrets are used to avoid the contention that your production techniques and equipment were common knowledge.

It is important to document the fact that you have a uniform policy of advising employees of the secret and confidential nature of your trade secrets, customer lists, and other information you wish protected. One way of doing this is to take minutes of regular meetings for all employees, at which such instructions are given. Another way is to have some document signed by employees as soon as they begin work; it should outline those production techniques, trade secrets, customer information, etc., which you regard as proprietary and confidential, and it should contain an acknowledgment that the employee has read the document and understands that such information is not to be disseminated during the employee's tenure with your organization or used or disseminated by the employee after completion of employment for whatever reason. In short, the more you can document and evidence the sensitive, proprietary, or confidential nature of your business, the better your chances when you take a disloyal employee to court.

There are some commonsense precautions that can also be taken. First, it is wise to keep sensitive information separate from your everyday files, which contain information of common knowledge. We advise keeping such information in locked file cabinets and giving keys to only your most trusted employees.

Second, sensitive information should be divulged within your organization only on a "need to know" basis. There is little reason for a technician to know the identities, buying histories, and personal preferences of your key customers. Conversely, it is probably unnecessary for sales personnel to have an intimate knowledge of detailed scientific information related to production rather than to quality of product. By operating on a need-to-know basis, you minimize the risks of one employee walking off with a knowledge of your entire organization.

Third, it is a good idea to be extra careful with employees who have indicated that they will be departing. If possible, "short-timers" should be kept away from sensitive areas, such as transactions of great importance to the organization and major accounts. It is a good idea to watch the hours of such short-timers to make sure that they are not "burning the midnight oil" in an effort to learn everything about your organization for disloyal reasons. In some industries in which piracy is rife, short-timers are either given an immediate leave or are rotated to areas of the business where they are not privy to sensitive materials. Such precautions are particularly in order when an employee has indicated that he will be leaving and has not indicated where he is going. In such instances, the safest course is to assume that he soon will be in the employ of your fiercest competitor.

To summarize this section: noncompetition agreements are a good idea in appropriate cases. To be enforceable, however, such agreements must be reasonable, both in time and in territory covered. Such agreements should spell out both injunctive relief and monetary damages. Where monetary damages are provided, care should be exercised to ensure that the clause will be regarded as liquidated damages (reasonably approximating the actual damages you will suffer), rather than as a penalty clause. In the absence of such agreements, company policies enunciating proprietary information and the company's desire to keep it secret should be instituted. The more such policies can be evidenced, particularly with regard to the fact that all employees were uniformly advised and treated, the better. Finally, there is no substitute for good common sense in protecting your proprietary information; keep it on a "need to know" basis and maintain elementary security procedures. This is not to say that you should run your organization in a suspicious manner akin to that of the Secret Service. A low-key, pleasant explanation of the need for security in a competitive business world need not turn your employees off. It is simply part of a well run business and should be presented as a reasonable means of assuring a secure, profitable environment for the benefit of everyone.

11

How Dealers and Distributors Can Handle Manufacturers

The law provides much more protection to the dealer or franchisee today than it did thirty years ago. There has been a tremendous increase in the number of damage awards for improper termination of franchises and in the fairness of interparty dealings.

When a manufacturer decides to get rid of a dealer or distributor, he is afraid of several things. First is the fear that he will be hit by an antitrust claim exposing him to treble damages or a government investigation. The discovery that the target dealer has in his possession a one-year-old letter from the regional sales manager complaining about price cutting by the dealer and threatening to do something if he doesn't stop has caused more than one large settlement to that dealer, or produced a very favorable continuing contract for him. So, save your price-fixing letters. Other sensitive subjects like this one include enforcement of territorial restraints, discriminatory pricing among competing dealers, discriminatory credit terms, or promotional allowances and the like. All of these practices are common and likely to be antitrust violations under either federal or state antitrust laws.

A complaint to the Federal Trade Commission, or threat thereof, is one way to get someone else to carry the burden of proving your case. However, the Federal Trade Commission gets so many complaints that it will seldom act unless you have a blatant case involving a large company. The regional offices in Chicago, Atlanta, and other cities have become more responsive than the Washington office in recent years. Certain state's attorney generals have become active in the antitrust area as well, and can be a source of help or advice.

Be advised that there are great differences in the awareness levels of this kind of claim among private attorneys. An attorney experienced in handling termination cases will get a great deal more mileage out of such claims than will the general practitioner, who is much more likely to focus on breach of contract matters.

The next great concern on the part of the manufacturer lies in liability for reliance damages. The manufacturer is exposed by recent cases to liability for investments in the business made by the dealer or distributor in the reasonable expectation that his contract would continue long enough to have a chance of recouping his investment. This point can be illustrated by two extreme examples:

1. No liability would be likely in the case of a distributor terminated—(a) at the end of five years; (b) in strict accordance with a year-to-year contract; (c) when six-month's, or more, notice of the impending termination had been given; (d) when the line was 10 percent of the business; (e) when no new, large investments had been made in facilities for this line; and (f) when all the other dealings had been fair.

2. Liability probably would result where—(a) the manufacturer signed a contract for one year; (b) the manufacturer prompted the distributor to build a new warehouse and buy new trucks or spend money developing the territory or suffer start-up losses; (c) the manufacturer's line was over 50 percent

of the distributor's volume; and (d) a thirty-day notice of cancellation was sent without good cause under the contract (the damage claim in this case could include the reasonably expected profits, if provable, and at least repayment of the last investment in the business).

An increasingly difficult area is the new franchise laws that have been adopted by nearly every jurisdiction. Contrary to what one might expect from the title, these laws often reach dealer and distributor termination cases as well. They can provide a basis for enjoining a termination and for collecting damages for wrongful termination.

One final word of caution in this area. There are far more dreams of large antitrust settlements than there are actual settlements. Use your weapons prudently for an attainable goal within the framework of your particular negotiation.

12

Contractual Disputes

Into the life of every business a little rain must fall—it seems. Conflict and dispute is almost inevitable in today's complex business world with its myriad competitive and financial pressures. Contracts which were thought to cover every eventuality when drafted turn out to be inadequate as time passes during the life of the agreement. The wise businessman expects a certain number of contractual disputes and knows what to do when they arise.

PRESERVING EVIDENCE

One of the most common complaints lawyers have when they are called in to resolve a business dispute is the inexplicable tendency on the part of their clients to fail to preserve evidence. Don't let this be your mistake. The watchword on preservation of evidence is "when in doubt, save it." This goes for pieces of evidence which would seem to be harmful as well as those which would seem to be helpful. Almost inevitably, the destruction of evidence by a client proves at least as fatal as preserving it and dealing with it in an intelligent way.

In court, a picture does "say a thousand words." Consequently, as machinery breaks down, paint peels, foundations heave, or any of the other multitudinous events in the area of physical facts occur, GET A PICTURE OF IT! If you make memoranda of telephone conversations, keep them in a file which is organized for such matters. If there is considerable money at stake, do not be niggardly about making a videotape. Dictate memoranda to yourself. When an important telephone call is made and there may be some doubt later as to what was said, advise the person you're speaking with that you are recording the conversation, and do so. When you are dealing with someone whom you don't quite trust, or when a highly sensitive matter is at hand, bring along an associate who can be a witness at a later date. When you have completed your conference, both you and your associate should make memoranda of what was said. Write letters confirming agreements which are made orally. Such letters needn't be formal and stiff, but should clearly state agreements that are made. We are not suggesting that you vastly increase the amount of paperwork involved in your business. We are strongly urging you, however, to evidence problems and highly important events in the history of your business. Photographs, memoranda, and letters at such times should not be too great a burden upon you, and can prove invaluable as time passes.

CREATING EVIDENCE

This section is suggested by the preceding one. As disputes begin to heat up, the prudent businessman does what he can to ensure that documentation and other evidence supporting his position exist at the earliest possible date. Without being wordy and overly legalistic, a letter explaining your position and inviting a reply is a good idea. If no reply is made, the arbiters of the facts and law at a later date will probably assume that the other side had no response at that time. If you do elicit a response, at least you have flushed out the other side's position so that you can deal with it intelligently.

This is the time when recordings of telephone conversations should be made and witnesses should be brought along to meetings. If the dispute is technical, experts can be brought in and studies can be made, which can be presented to the other side. Once again, reponses, or failures to respond, can prove extremely significant if you have to go to court or arbitration.

Thought should be given to the employment of investigators in appropriate cases. One word here: it is a good idea to consult with your attorney before hiring an investigator, since some of them are not particularly reliable or reputable. If you do not consult with an attorney to find a reliable investigator, we recommend that you get a clear-cut (preferably written) understanding of the terms under which you are hiring the investigator; particularly with regard to his hourly rates, costs, and expenses. Care should be taken not to involve yourself in "cloak and dagger" type operations with investigators, which, if revealed at a later date, can be more harmful than helpful. Remember the embarrassment suffered by General Motors when Ralph Nadar blew the whistle on their "super sleuth"? The best investigators go about their business in an extremely innocuous, businesslike way. If possible, avoid investigators who tend to flirt with the privacy laws, electronic eavesdropping laws, and unlawful entry laws.

You can do a great deal of the investigating yourself, utilizing the telephone, utilizing financial services, inquiring of bankers and other knowledgeable parties, and befriending persons close to the other side. Disgruntled ex-employees are often marvelous sources of information. If, when a dispute is brewing, you find witnesses, such as disgruntled ex-employees and other persons who deal with the other side, be sure that you pin such witnesses down by a signed letter or statement, a tape recording, or a verbatim statement taken down by a court reporter. Your lawyer can help you regarding how to make such statements and how to ensure that they will be valid and usable in court. One way is to put the statement in the form of an affidavit. Affidavits are easily created instruments and require only a notary to validate them. You may well have a notary working for you in your business. If not, most banks and insurance offices have notaries available. The following is an example of an affidavit:

STATE OF MINNESOTA

ss.   *AFFIDAVIT OF*

COUNTY OF CAMELOT   *DENNIS DISGRUNTLED*

DENNIS DISGRUNTLED, being first duly sworn on oath, deposes and states:

That your affiant was formerly the production supervisor for the Ace Mucket Company; that your affiant left its employ on November 3, 1978; that during the month of October, 1978, your affiant had occasion to deal with numerous breakdowns of the Ace Mucket assembly line; that during such break-downs, Ace Mucket was preparing muckets for the Peerless Plaintiff, Inc., account; that your affiant called to the attention of the president of the Ace Mucket Company the fact that the muckets which were being made for Peerless during the breakdowns were of inferior quality; that the president of the company advised your affiant to keep silent about the inferior muckets and to mix them in with good muckets in the packages which were sent to Peerless; that your affiant pro-tested about the dishonesty of doing this and was subsequently fired for failing to obey orders; that your affiant knows from first-hand observation that the inferior muckets were sent to Peerless by direct order of Ace's president.

FURTHER YOUR AFFIANT SAYETH NOT.

Signed: _____

Dated: _____

(Notarization clause and stamp affixed)

NEGOTIATION OF DISPUTES

It has been said that "a bad settlement is better than a good lawsuit." Factors militating in favor of settlement as opposed to litigation are numerous. Some of the most important are the following: (1) the cost of litigation (and even arbitration) as opposed to working things out between the parties; (2) the delays involved in getting the matter on for hearing in court or arbitration; (3) the uncertainty involved in placing the fate of your business in the hands of a judge or a jury rather than working it out by negotiation yourself; (4) the chance of making enemies of people that you have to get along with in the future; (5) the amount of attention and time (both your own and that of your key employees) that litigation will absorb; (6) the money you will lose in the form of lost production; and (7) the very unpleasantness of fighting about something—who knows, negotiating a dispute may save you an ulcer operation in the future!

Assuming that you have a dispute or disagreement with at least one other party, how should you go about handling it? If you are going to negotiate, we strongly recommend having a definite, preconceived strategy as opposed to simply picking up the telephone or dashing off a letter without giving any further thought as to what you seek to accomplish. Preliminary to devising a strategy, it is important to preserve your evidence and, if possible, create evidence along the lines suggested in the first two sections of this chapter. Once you have done this, it is important to become as informed as possible about both the facts and the law involved in the dispute. The latter will probably mean consultation with your lawyer before you begin bargaining. It is simply not wise to begin bargaining about a dispute without knowing the legal ramifications of what you are bargaining for. Further, it is literally impossible to negotiate effectively without knowing all the facts that might come up. Consequently, it seems obvious that you should get the actual facts and law mapped out in advance. We cannot emphasize the importance of doing this before contacting your opposition.

Next, it is important to understand your adversary. Try to "psych him out" by taking a thoughtful look at the size and relative strength of his business, the pressures upon him as a businessman, the nature of his business, and his personality. Generally, the maxim "You draw more flies with honey than with vinegar" is true. Consequently, if the president of the company you are going to negotiate with is a devout Seventh Day Adventist, it is unwise to attempt to schedule a meeting with him on Saturday morning. There is no way you can know this unless you make some inquiry about the person with whom you are going to be dealing.

There are times when a hard line is better than a soft approach. The important thing is to determine whether this is necessary, given the nature of your opposition. Sometimes, a blend of the two approaches can be taken by using a negotiating team comprised of a hard-liner and a soft-liner. Under such a format, negotiations can be opened with the tough guy taking a hard stance and the conciliatory member of the team mollifying the opposition a little later—after the hard-liner has sounded them out. Lawyers frequently employ this tactic when they utilize a litigator and a business lawyer in an attempt to negotiate a dispute. First, the litigator points out to the other side the probably disastrous consequences of trying the case. After he has shaken the other side out of their complacency, the business lawyer can sit down and explain the practicalities of settlement as opposed to litigation, proposing some alternative settlement plans with different tax ramifications, etc.

It is sometimes a good idea to keep the president of the company or persons with ultimate authority in the background. Thus, time can be gained because no one will have to leave the bargaining table to get in contact with the party in authority. This allows time to regroup and to make counteroffers without insulting the opposition by flatly turning down their offers at the bargaining table.

Once you have determined what your overall strategy is, have educated yourself as to the facts and the law, have determined whether you are going to take a hard or soft stance, and have set up your negotiating group, or team, it is important to consider the various alternatives and hammer out your probable proposals. In the experience of the authors, it is best to have several alternatives. This involves carefully evaluating your position and coming up with a probable range of results in the event you have to take the matter to litigation. Thus, you will have assessed the situation so as to determine the best *likely* result if you go to court (taking care to subtract the costs of litigation) as well as the worst *probable* result. Once you have done this, you can determine the probabilities of winning or losing and come up with a *reasonable* range of settlement. Once you have done this, it is a good idea to prepare proposals, preferably in writing, outlining an excellent result, a medium satisfactory result, and the least acceptable result you are willing to live with short of going to court. It is not recommended that any of these be disclosed to your opposition at any time before arriving at a settlement. You shouldn't even reveal that you will accept several alternatives. Once a settlement has been arrived at, however, it is very nice to be able to "close" promptly, before your opposition has a chance to go back and change its mind. Once again, the merits of advance preparation are very apparent.

Sometimes, particularly in fields involving heavy technology, it is a good idea to bring to the negotiations a third party, preferably one who is somewhat expert, and supposedly neutral, but who happens to agree with your side of the dispute. Sometimes the other side will listen to such an "expert" at a time when they will not listen to you.

When negotiating a dispute, the key to success is preparation. The tax ramifications, accounting ramifications, and all other business aspects should be thought out in advance. Further, the goals and psychology of your opposition should be plumbed as deeply as possible. Such goals may very well be compatible with your own in many respects. This will enable you to point out your common ground, rather than hitting your opposition in the face with your conflicts at the outset. Certainly, both you and your opposition have a common goal of wishing to maximize your profits and minimize your losses. It well may be that a comparison of goals of your businesses, done in a calm and rational manner, will result in the discovery of common ground where you can agree.

Sometimes it is not a good idea to bring accountants or lawyers to negotiations, particularly if your accountant or your lawyer tends to be overly technical. The important thing, in the same theme of preparation, is to make sure that you have given thought to who ought to be at the negotiation and who is going to take what role and say what; this will prevent you from getting your signals confused during sensitive negotiations.

Finally, in addition to the foregoing grounds for consulting your lawyer before negotiation, another one is to get advice as to whether you should do something in advance of negotiation to ensure that things that are said in negotiation are not used against you later. Remember, the very negotiation process may be evidence at a later trial or arbitration. Care should be taken that you do not create evidence unfavorable to yourself. The ultimate in stupidity would be to make some damaging admission such as "I know I owe you x dollars but you will probably have to sue me to get it, and that will cost you a lot of money and delay." Such an admission would obviously be disastrous in court. While few negotiators would be foolish enough to make such a flagrant admission, there are other things which perhaps should be avoided during the negotiating process so as not to render your litigating position impossible in the event negotiations break down. If disclosures of some sort must be made, you may make a signed agreement stipulating that whatever is discussed during negotiations will not be admissible in any later case between the parties. This is where consultation with a lawyer before negotiation becomes an excellent idea.

ARBITRATION

With the increasing backlog in the courts, arbitration has

become more popular. Arbitration can be had either by mutual consent after a dispute has arisen, or in accordance with a contract or charter of a trade association. An example of the latter instance is the New York Stock Exchange; all disputes among its members are determined by arbitration conducted by specialists at the Stock Exchange.

This points up one of the merits of having an arbitration clause, thereby insuring that arbitration is the means of settling a dispute rather than the courts; arbitration is private, and no public record is made for reporters and the general public to view. Another advantage of arbitration is that experts decide the dispute instead of laymen or judges who have no particular expertise. This is particularly desirable in high-technology areas. Another potential advantage is that seldom, if ever, do arbitrators allow prehearing discovery such as depositions, interrogatories, and document productions. Occasionally arbitration can be had by application to court, if there is a state statute (about thirty states have such statutes) whereby parties can apply for court-supervised arbitration. Generally, however, parties will not be delayed or otherwise inconvenienced by having to submit to depositions, interrogatories, or any of the other discovery tools that trial lawyers employ.

Another possible advantage of arbitration is that arbitrators will not be reversed even if they make some errors of law in arriving at their conclusions. The idea behind this is that arbitration is supposed to be final and not subject to appeals to higher courts. So, if you have a dispute in which you feel the overall equities are in your favor but some niggling provision of the law might cause you to lose, you are better off in arbitration. The converse is also true; that is, if some rather fine point of the law supports your position (perhaps an evidentiary point that would cause some evidence that is harmful to you to be inadmissible in court), you are better off refusing arbitration and insisting upon going to court.

Arbitration is usually faster for a relatively small dispute. However, since arbitrators are not regularly sitting judges, if the dispute is very complex and likely to take many days of hearings, arbitration may not be quicker, since you may find yourself having to take the arbitrators when they are available. Frequently, experts, such as those used in a typical arbitration, are very busy men and can only meet occasionally. If this is the case, arbitration can drag on for weeks or months. The entire idea of arbitration is speed and economy. It was never designed to handle the major disputes of the times.

One of the disadvantages of arbitration is a certain loss of control as a result of turning the dispute entirely over to experts, who have the freedom to be somewhat erroneous in the application of law. Before doing this, care should be exercised in making sure that the experts do not have a bias which can harm you. Some experts are very opinionated in their expertise. The only way an expert arbitrator's opinion in an arbitration can be overturned is if it can be demonstrated that the arbitrator was deliberately prejudiced to the point of being arbitrary and capricious in his judgment or that the arbitration itself was somehow tainted by dishonesty, fraud, and the like. By going to arbitration, one gives up some of the protections of the law—protections which can be very comforting in the event of error.

An advantage, or disadvantage, of arbitration, depending on how you look at it, is the fact that the rules of evidence are completely relaxed in arbitration. Hearsay evidence can be brought in, witnesses can appear by affidavit rather than being present (and therefore available for cross-examination), documentary evidence that is not the "best evidence" may be introduced, and the arbitrators are allowed to consider nearly anything they wish. This is fine as long as you have very strong faith in the arbitrators.

The authors recommend a "broad" arbitration clause in a contract, if one is to be included, rather than a "narrow" clause limiting arbitration to certain items. Such narrow clauses have a way of causing the arbitration itself to go to court in a fight over whether an item is arbitrable. This generally defeats the very purpose of arbitration—speed and economy. An example of a broad clause, recommended by the American Arbitration Association, is as follows:

> Any controversy or claim arising out of or relating to this contract, or the breach thereof, shall be settled by arbitration in accordance with the commercial arbitration rules of the American Arbitration Association, and judgment upon the award rendered by the arbitrator(s) may be entered in any court having jurisdiction thereof.

Obviously, this arbitration clause could easily be tailored to handle arbitration by other arbitrators. In addition, the American Arbitration Association has a recommended clause for the submission of existing disputes. It reads as follows:

> We, the undersigned parties, hereby agree to submit to arbitration under the Commercial Arbitration Rules of the American Arbitration Association the following controversy: (cite briefly). We further agree that the above controversy be submitted to (1) (3) arbitrator(s) selected by the panels of arbitrators of the American Arbitration Association. We further agree that we will faithfully observe this agreement and the rules and that we will abide by and perform any award rendered by the arbitrator(s) and that a judgment of the court having jurisdiction may be entered upon the award.

CONTRACT LITIGATION

An entire book could be devoted to the trial of a contract case. Indeed, in the authors' offices, a very large percentage of all litigation is contract litigation for businessmen. Entire textbooks and law school courses are devoted to only the damages aspect of litigation, others to the liability aspect. There are, nevertheless, a few general considerations which should be brought out in this book.

First, since litigation is costly, a party considering involvement should weigh the costs. This involves not only determining whether you can afford the litigation, but also a comparison of your economic strength relative to that of your opposition. If your opponent has greater financial resources than you, a careful assessment of the costs and a long conference with your attorney regarding the disparity in economic position between you and your opponent should be held. If possible, you should get an estimate of the cost and time involved in litigating.

Second, the delay factor should not be ignored. Does time weigh for or against you? This is another subject to bring up with your lawyers. The court calendar backlog varies greatly across the country depending on whether you are in federal court, state court, or municipal court. A reasonable forecast of the delay before your case can be heard and a judgment obtained and collected should be made before embarking on litigation.

Third, you should try to arrive at an estimate of how well prepared you are for litigation. Factors such as how much emotional upset is involved, how disruptive it will be to your business organization (particularly considering the modern tendency toward a great amount of discovery, such as deposition, document production, interrogatories), how important it is to keep secret the aspects of your business that will of necessity be revealed, the effect upon related businesses and individuals who may have to be witnesses, the availability of evidence, whether your business has sufficient cash reserves, and many other factors must be weighed with regard to preparedness.

Finally, an accurate assessment of how a judge or jury will perceive your case should be obtained from an objective party, such as an attorney. There is an old saying among attorneys when it comes to clients wishing to "fight for the principle involved": "I will be happy to fight for your principles down to *your* last penny." This is not to say that the authors are cynical about fighting for one's principles, even when the odds are slim. Occasionally, regardless of the odds, it is important to make a stand. But before you charge off jousting at legal windmills in the name of principle, be certain that you assess the costs!

In the authors' experience, businessmen, because of the

uncertainties involved in trying cases, like to fight right down to the courthouse steps, keeping the risks assessed at all times and attempting to make the best possible deal at the best possible time. There is nothing wrong with this process; sometimes the only way to truly assess the situation is to commence a lawsuit and embark upon discovery. With capable counsel involved, once the discovery process has been initiated and a great deal more learned about the facts and the application of pertinent law, a much more intelligent solution can be found than at the time the battle lines were first drawn. Most successful businessmen are pragmatic. Once they have learned as much as they can about the situation, have had the risks assessed and a range of probable result presented, they will opt to at least attempt a settlement. Of course, if the opposition is unwilling to even consider settlement within the probable range of result, the case should probably be tried. Once one has gone through the process of assessing the risks, attempting to discuss and resolve the matter amicably, and has been turned down, it is much easier to justify bringing the case to trial.

13

A Word on Hiring and Working with Lawyers

As in medicine and many other fields, the age of specialization is upon us in law. Although by no means obsolete, the general practitioner is increasingly becoming a lawyer who identifies the nature of the problem and refers it to the appropriate specialist. What does this mean to the businessman? Clearly, it means that he must become more sophisticated than his counterpart of twenty-five years ago. Unfortunately, not all lawyers are willing to relinquish control over a client, even when they know that there are lawyers more skilled than themselves in addressing specific problems. On the one hand, much is to be said for staying with a lawyer who is familiar with your business. However, much is also to be said for insisting upon top-notch expertise from the lawyer entrusted with finding the solution to a specific problem.

Because of the need for specialization and the further need to provide the American businessman with "one stop" service, the full service law firm, comprised of specialists in nearly every field encountered by businessmen, has evolved in recent years. Your authors are probably biased in favor of such a firm, since they belong to one. We believe that from the viewpoint of the businessman, it is best to have a regular association with a group of lawyers capable of directing specific expertise to nearly any problem the businessman is likely to encounter. This enables the client to enjoy the familiarity of one organization, which is aware of him as a valuable, continuing account, is knowledgeable about the history of his business, yet is able to direct specialized knowledge to his specific problems.

If you do not establish a relationship with a full service law firm, the authors recommend that you establish a relationship with a general practitioner who is not so jealous of specialists that he will retain your work in areas where he has limited expertise. You should not have to pay to educate your lawyer about an area of the law with which he is unfamiliar. You have a perfect right to assume that the lawyer you retain for any problem is experienced in dealing, if not with the specific problem, at least with the field within which the problem rests. The only way to learn this is to inquire specifically about the extent of the lawyer's familiarity with problems of the type in question. If you are unsatisfied with the answer you receive, you should not feel embarrassed about inquiring of others who the top people in the field are. To reiterate, the first step in retaining a lawyer to handle a legal problem for you is to find out whether the lawyer is skilled in handling that specific type of problem.

Another early consideration is cost. Your authors firmly recommend getting the matter of fees worked out as early as possible. Regardless of the kind of fee to be charged for the services, it is important to establish a firm understanding of how the fee will be charged and to obtain as accurate a prediction as possible of its amount. This can save some very nasty surprises later on. Upon first discussing a matter with a lawyer, do not be shy about pressing for an answer to all questions you have concerning fees. Neither you nor your lawyer want you leaving his office with a misunderstanding about fees.

Generally, there are four ways lawyers charge fees: hourly fees, retainers, fees based upon the reasonable value of the services, and contingent fees.

Hourly Fees

If your lawyer is going to charge you by the hour, the authors recommend that you exhibit a bit more sophistication than simply learning what the lawyer's hourly rate is. Appearances can be very deceptive when it comes to hourly fees. It seems that an hour is not the same in all law firms. Some law firms are known to quote rather low hourly rates, but when compared with the costs of other lawyers who quote higher hourly rates, the final fee for a given item of work is often as high or higher from the lawyer who quotes the low hourly rate. Why is this so? One reason is that some law firms require, or set a policy strongly recommending, that all of their lawyers obtain a certain minimum number of hours billed per day. This causes the lawyers in such firms to simply allocate all of the hours in the day to specific clients whom they worked for during a given day, without regard to the actual number of minutes spent on each client's case. With such firms, you may very well find yourself paying for part of the time the lawyer spent strolling back and forth from the coffee station!

Further, some law firms are more efficient than others in delegating their work to lower paid associates, secretaries, and paraprofessionals. Clearly, the more work that can be performed by lower paid employees of the law office, such as paralegals, who do not have law degrees but have great expertise in specific areas, the lower your overall average hourly rate will be.

What can you do to achieve greater sophistication in the tricky area of hourly fees? The authors recommend that before you hire a lawyer or law firm, you inquire specifically into the following areas: (a) how the lawyer uses paraprofessionals; (b) whether he blocks his time for an entire day or "stops his meter" when he is not working on a specific problem; and (c) most importantly, particularly if you are seeking to establish a permanent relationship with a lawyer or law firm for your business, ask other businessmen about the reasonableness of a specific firm's fees. The important thing to remember is that the simple quotation of an hourly rate can be very misleading.

One final word: it is possible to be penny-wise and pound-foolish here. Do not expect to obtain a Mercedes for the price of a Ford. Generally, lawyers, like other providers of services to the businessman, base their charges on what they are worth. There are notable exceptions, however, and this is the reason we recommend some comparison shopping and independent inquiry before retaining a lawyer or law firm.

Another way to check into your lawyer's abilities is to find out who some of the lawyer's clients are. There is a volume called the Martindale-Hubbell Law Directory available in most law libraries and some public libraries. Nearly all law libraries and law offices have a set of Martindale-Hubbell directories. In Martindale-Hubbell you can find biographical sketches of the members of most leading law firms and lawyers in each state, broken down city by city. Among the items listed for each law firm are some of its representative clients. These are ideal sources to check out in determining whether the lawyer or law firm you are considering is a good one for you.

Retainers

Some lawyers and clients prefer to establish an arrangement based upon a retainer fee. There are at least two different types of retainers. One kind is a fee that is paid to a law firm to keep that law firm retained as the client's firm, available for consultation on short notice without any further arrangements. The concept involved in such a fee is an understanding that by periodic payment of a rather substantial fee, the client has ensured that that lawyer or law firm will be available for any problem the client encounters and asks for legal services about. Thus, the law firm or lawyer is "retained" for the needs of the client.

You may be surprised to learn that there are some law firms and lawyers who will not consider doing any work for a new client until a substantial retainer fee has been paid. In the authors' experience, this is much more typical of some of the most famous law firms in the country and is not prevalent throughout the United States. Such firms already have as many good clients as they can comfortably handle, and the only basis upon which they will take new clients is if the client pays a very substantial retainer in advance. Happily for the consumer of legal services, this is not the situation nationwide; the legal services market is much more of a buyer's than a seller's market.

Another kind of retainer is the retainer insisted upon by a law firm or lawyer before it will begin handling a given case or legal problem. Such retainers are usually not paid just for the privilege of having the lawyer on retention but are actually advance payments of fees. When such a retainer is paid, the lawyer usually works on the case or problem until he nears the point where he has exhausted the amount of the retainer. Under most such arrangements, the lawyer then insists upon another advance retainer to keep him working on the problem or case.

In the field of criminal law, lawyers nearly always insist upon getting their fees "up front" in this manner. However, in criminal law, the lawyer nearly always gets the entire fee, agreed upon in advance, paid before he begins work. The reason is obvious: upon completion of the work, the client may be going to jail and totally unable, or unwilling, to pay a fee!

You may be asking yourself, what is the reason for making any mention in a book of this nature of representation in criminal cases? The short answer is that businessmen are sometimes accused of committing crimes. Indeed, in the

authors' experience, many business clients have found themselves worrying about criminal laws and regulations that they
never dreamed existed! This is another good reason for
maintaining a working relationship with a law firm. The
authors have represented businessmen who have run afoul of
the criminal provisions of the securities law when they didn't
even have an idea they were dealing with "securities." Tax
fraud is not uncommon in a business context. There are
criminal provisions in the labor, environmental, and occupa-
tional fields, to mention a few. Although the authors certainly
do not regard themselves as criminal lawyers, nor any of their
business clients as criminals, the same considerations come
into play when representing a businessman charged with a
crime as anyone else. In all likelihood, if the lawyer does not
request payment of all fees in advance, he is at least going to
require a substantial retainer to work against in the event of
criminal prosecution. In such a case, the businessman charged
with the crime should not be timid in negotiating the fee.

Trial lawyers commonly work against retainers in this
manner, particularly where there is substantial risk of losing
the case. Once again, the reason is obvious: if the case is lost,
there is likely to be considerable disappointment regardless of
how well the lawyer has performed, and, consequently, there
is substantial risk of a fee dispute unless the fee has been paid
in advance. Another reason for advance retainers in the area of
trial practice is that judges are not always willing to allow
lawyers to withdraw from cases they have begun handling
because the client has become delinquent in paying fees.

According to the Canons of Ethics, unless there is a written
agreement permitting withdrawal for nonpayment of fees,
worked out in advance, it is not ethical for a lawyer to
withdraw from a case simply because the client has become
unable to pay. Usually, withdrawal can be effected, but it is
sticky for the lawyer and requires an appearance in court and
a showing that the withdrawal is not going to prejudice the
client's rights in an unfair manner and that the nonpayment
of fees is unwarranted on the part of the client. This can put

the lawyer in a real bind. In order to avoid such a situation, advance retainers are called for, particularly from someone who is not a long-standing client of the law firm or lawyer.

Where a long-term relationship has been established, most law firms and lawyers will handle contested matters on a straight hourly basis, or other arrangement, without insisting upon an advance retainer. If your business is one with frequent disputes, this is another good reason to find a law firm capable of handling all of your work. Its members will become "your lawyers," familiar with your business, and available to go to work for you on contested matters without haggling over fees as each matter comes up.

A word of warning here: if your business does not normally become embroiled in contested cases but you find yourself confronted with one, even though your relationship with your lawyers has been very smooth up to this point, it is a good idea to go in and work out a firm understanding with the lawyer who is going to handle the contested case. The authors strongly recommend that before the case is started you get an estimate of probable cost, and that you follow the progress of the case closely. Ask the lawyer upon the completion of each step how many more steps there are likely to be and what is his *current* estimate of the amount of work and fees necessary to complete the case.

It is very difficult to predict the cost of a complicated piece of litigation in which many of the moves that can be made are up to the other side. Your lawyer is going to be hard-pressed to predict accurately, at the very start of litigation, how many depositions his opponent will decide to take, how many sets of interrogatories will be served upon him by his opponent, how many motions will be brought before the court during the history of the case, etc. However, as he works his way into the case, he will obtain a better feel for how hard the opposition is going to fight, and his estimates of costs will probably become more accurate. So it is a good idea to continue the estimating process as you go along, while you are involved in the lawsuit. This is also a good idea when you're working through any very complicated problem with a lawyer. Neither side likes surprises when it comes to receiving and rendering billings for legal services.

Reasonable Value Billing

Some lawyers and clients, particularly after they have established a good working relationship, prefer billings on a "reasonable value" basis. That is, the lawyer renders a bill upon the completion of a job, if it is small enough, or periodically if it is a long-term job, based upon the lawyer's estimate of the fair value of the services provided. This allows the lawyer to do some extra billing for exceptionally good results and allows him the latitude to reduce his fee below the normal value of his time if a bad result is obtained. Such fees were much more common in former days, when there were more sole practitioners who were not answerable to other partners in their firm for each hour of their time. However, many modern law firms allow their lawyers latitude to adjust bills below or above hourly rates according to results, particularly in case of bad results for clients of long standing and of considerable value to the firm.

Although it probably seems too obvious to mention, like all human beings, lawyers make mistakes. Perhaps because they are expected to be smart, however, some lawyers are inclined to perpetuate a myth of infallibility. Most good lawyers mellow a bit as they become more experienced and make some mistakes; they become more willing to admit it when they drop the ball. It is not fair to insist upon infallibility from a lawyer any more than from anyone else who provides goods or services to your business. However, it is reasonable to expect adjustments in fees because of mistakes, if you are also willing to pay extra for exceptional work. Lawyers commonly do not charge time-and-a-half or double time for overtime, yet they are frequently called upon to give advice on Sundays, holidays, and at night. Sometimes they accomplish little miracles because of some inspiration they get while handling a matter.

It seems fair that they should be rewarded for extraordinary services, particularly if they are willing to reduce fees for achieving results that are less than estimated or expected.

As stated above, results billing is more common when the lawyer and client have worked out over a period of time a relationship that allows for it. A certain amount of trust is required between lawyer and client before a results billing arrangement will work. The client has to become comfortable with the fees charged by the lawyer so that he doesn't feel that he is going to be gouged for fees vastly in excess of the amount of time the lawyer has put in on the job, simply because there was no flat agreement predicated upon hours or an earlier estimate. Likewise, the lawyer has to be sufficiently comfortable with the relationship to know that the client will not be in his office fighting about the amount of the bill every time he receives one.

Contingent Fees

Contingent fees are very common in the area of personal injury litigation. A contingent fee is a fee which will only be received by the law firm or lawyer if a given result is achieved. In personal injury litigation, very typically the contingent fee is one-third of all amounts collected, plus the lawyer's out-of-pocket costs involved in handling the case. The out-of-pocket costs are usually not part of the contingent fee and must be paid regardless of the result.

Contingent fees are also frequently worked out for collections. Normally, when a business turns over bad accounts for collection, it is not interested in "throwing good money after bad," and therefore is only willing to pay fees out of amounts collected. The percentages charged for collections are frequently on a sliding scale based upon the size of the account. Obviously, a million dollar collection can probably be handled for a much smaller percentage than a $500 matter. In some rare instances, the authors have even heard of one hundred percent contingent fees occurring when the debtor is a real deadbeat but the creditor wants him pursued because of the principle involved, even though there is no real hope of collecting anything for himself. Contingent fee arrangements for collection usually provide for withdrawal in the event that the lawyer determines, in his judgment, that the account is uncollectible because of insolvency or other reasons.

Sometimes contingent fees are set up on two levels, such as 25 percent of all amounts collected if the case is settled before going to court and 33 percent if the case actually goes to trial.

The philosophy behind contingent fees is that everyone is entitled to representation and should not be prevented from asserting a meritorious claim because of inability to finance legal representation. Consequently, the American legal system allows attorneys to have a stake in the outcome of the case. Some people believe the concept of a stake in the outcome of the case also tends to prevent lawyers from undertaking worthless causes. On the other hand, it can be argued with equal force that once a lawyer has invested considerable time on a case, he may be less inclined to drop it in the event it appears worthless somewhere down the line. In any event, contingent fees are generally acceptable in United States courts with one exception: it is generally unethical for a lawyer to undertake a criminal defense on a contingent basis.

Regardless of the type of fee arrived at, we recommend obtaining answers to all questions before representation is undertaken and reducing the understanding to writing. Most law firms have various standard form fee arrangements, or letters of retention, spelling out the important details concerning fees and the terms of representation. Such agreements benefit both the lawyer and client, and it is a wise client who requests a written agreement in the event the lawyer does not offer one. Disputes because of misunderstandings over fees and the terms of representation are always unpleasant, and the bad feelings which arise from such disputes can affect how your lawyer feels about you and your case, and, ultimately, the quality of representation you receive.

Another general word of advice in dealing with lawyers: do

not be reluctant to tell your lawyer the entire truth. You should remember that communications with a lawyer who is retained to work for you are privileged and cannot be discovered by anyone. This assumes, of course, that the lawyer is professional about keeping his mouth shut. Most lawyers, particularly those with any experience at all, have learned to keep confidences to themselves. The reason behind the need to tell the entire truth, no matter how embarrassing, is simply that the representation will be much more effective if the lawyer knows the whole story. Nothing is worse than a nasty surprise during trial or after a lawyer has begun representing a client on a mistaken assumption. Modern discovery methods permit inquiry into, and discovery of, facts and related circumstances that the client probably never dreams of. Your lawyer is supposed to be a trained professional, including the ability to keep confidences. You have a right to insist that he does so. If he is too good a friend to learn all the facts without embarrassing you, request and obtain a lawyer who is not in such a position. The important thing is to arm your lawyer with as complete and truthful a picture as possible. The adage "The truth shall make you free" can sometimes have a very literal meaning when it comes to working with lawyers!

14

Tips about Your Insurance Protection

BUYING INSURANCE PROTECTION

This chapter will not deal with the whole range of insurance protection, such as health and life insurance plans for your company. Rather, the considerations in this chapter are confined to liability insurance, which protects you from the negligence cases that might be brought against you, product liability cases, and insurance on your buildings, vehicles, inventory, and property. Generally, this type of insurance is called liability insurance.

In buying such insurance, as with nearly anything else, it is possible to be too thrifty. Insurance companies can be classified as high-class, middle-class, and bottom-of-the-line, just like nearly any other product or service that you might buy. To further confuse the issue, some insurance companies seem to take different attitudes in different parts of the country. Thus, for example, the claims office for the State Farm Insurance agency in one city may be dreadfully cheap when it comes to paying off claims; whereas another one may be very generous. How can this be? Don't insurance companies set national policies? Indeed they do. However, in addition to national policies, different claims departments in different locations reflect the personalities of their managers. All of these managers are concerned with one thing above all else: the bottom line—cost-effectiveness of their operations. In some locations, the branch manager may decide that it really pays to dispute nearly all claims, thereby reducing the amount the company pays out. In another section of the country, the manager of the entire branch office may be concerned with building the company's image; consequently, he instructs the claims manager to be generous on claims in order to obtain a larger share of the insurance market. Further, companies differ from time to time on a national level, sometimes paying off with very little fuss, and sometimes investigating and contesting nearly every claim. This is because different changes in the economy dictate the degree to which a given insurance company may wish to seek new business by accommodating the insurance buying public.

Faced with such a shifting set of variables, what is the businessman to do? Once again, the best policy when in doubt is discovered through research. Talk to contemporaries in your field to determine whether they are having satisfactory experiences with given companies. Invite the companies to prove themselves to you. Get your agent to obtain quotations from competing companies and make them justify their quotations on price with further justification of their record of promptness in paying claims, the percentage of claims which are paid, and other relevant statistics. All companies keep such records, and when prompted, if they want your business, will produce them. Make as many comparisons as you can, and get your agent to work for you. Indeed, obtain as many positive statements of coverage from both your agent and the quoting companies as you can. When buying insurance, try to become as sophisticated as you can about the different policy provisions that apply to your company. You won't regret it.

Another point to check out is the company's procedure for verifying and making claims. All companies have claims forms, but some make the claimant seem a common criminal who is suspected of lying from the outset; while others are relatively straightforward. A comparison of forms can be helpful in determining how difficult the company is likely to be when it comes to making a claim.

Remember one thing: no matter how cheap your insurance is, it is useless to you if the company won't pay off when you make a legitimate claim. And as a good businessman, you know the importance of cash flow. Consequently, the company's record of promptness in paying claims can be vitally important to you. Force the company that sells insurance to you to prove itself in these regards before buying. If your agent cannot come up with several alternative companies from which to choose, he may be overly involved with one company. A truly independent agent is a requisite to making an intelligent choice of insurers.

Amount of Coverage

How much coverage do you need? In today's world of greater and greater jury awards, the safest route when in doubt is to increase your limits. There are few states in the country where personal injury and product liability awards in a given case have not exceeded $1 million. In some states, such as New York, California, and Florida, verdicts of such size are common. Once again, a good agent can be helpful here, providing you with statistical data that is compiled by the insurance industry. Do not be satisfied with the agent's bald assertion that a certain amount of coverage is adequate if it isn't backed by statistical proof. A claim in excess of your insurance coverage, if successfully prosecuted, can result in the bankruptcy of your business.

Multiple Insurers

Be careful when you are using multiple insurance companies to make certain that there are no "gaps" between coverages. Your authors have recently been working with a company which, because of a slipup by an agent, found itself faced with a $150,000 gap between the amount of coverage provided by one insurer of the company and the next, "umbrella," insurance carrier. Your agent should periodically review your coverages to make certain that there are no gaps and that you are fully protected in light of inflation, etc. It is a good idea to set a certain date each year for a thorough review of your insurance coverages.

Perils Insured Against

In addition to amounts of coverage, it is necessary to know what perils you are insured against. This is the area in which writing of an insurance policy sometimes becomes a fine art. If you are not careful, you may think you are covered for your business, only to find that the insurance company has written coverage *out* of your policy for just the type of accident or calamity most likely to occur! A skilled agent, with expertise in your particular industry, is a real asset in buying insurance, both for recommending amounts of coverage and for making certain that all of the perils that could beset you are insured against. It is the authors' belief that to be truly effective, the agent should be both expert in your industry and sufficiently independent so that he is not allied with only one company. Any way you look at it, you'll be spending a considerable amount of money for insurance coverage. This being the case, you have every right to insist on the very best coverage for your insurance dollar.

Type of Insurance Company

A word should be said about the size and type of company. Some of the authors' worst experiences in attempting to collect claims for clients have arisen with small, mutual companies. It seems that the claims agents for some such companies are so involved in ownership that they feel as though allowance of a claim is payment of money out of their own pocket! The insurance commissions of some states, in the authors' opinion, permit companies to begin writing insurance with woefully inadequate capital behind them. The large, national stock companies are generally a safer bet. This is not to say, however, that the policy of a national insurance company, at a given time in a given place, will not be extremely parsimonious. In today's world of mounting claims, however, it is best to be on the safe side and go with a large, well-funded insurance company whenever possible.

DEALING WITH AGENTS

Few people realize how easy it is to make an insurance contract. The case law of most states is replete with instances of the courts finding coverage to exist for a loss that the insurance company denied. In general, if you call a registered agent of an insurance company and tell him, on the telephone, to cover a vehicle, building, or yourself for a given loss, etc., and he agrees to do so, you not only have legal rights against the agent if he fails to place the coverage, you also have a binding insurance contract with the company! The legal principles involved in this are simple: once you establish that an agent is indeed the agent of an insurance company, the deals he makes are also the insurance company's. Since commerce demands that insurance contracts be bound telephonically in many instances, with confirmation to come later, the law will generally support an oral contract to insure of the type alluded to above. The lesson to be learned from this for the businessman is clear: if you have talked with your agent about coverage for a given loss and you experience one, do not give up on your claim just because the insurance company, in the first instance, denies it on the basis of the nonexistence of a written policy: if you have made *any* arrangements for coverage, whether or not they were ever confirmed in writing with a binder, letter, or sending of a policy, do not give up on your claims. Go see a lawyer if you receive a denial in such a case. You may be pleasantly surprised.

This is not to say that you should not get documentary confirmation. The authors recommend, whenever coverage is placed by telephone or word of mouth, that documentation be created. Thus, as soon as you get off the telephone, drop your agent a brief letter confirming the conversation. If the coverage is big and very important to your business, a telegram is recommended so that the agent cannot claim that he did not receive word from you in time. Sometimes a coverage question can turn on a matter of hours, or minutes, rather than days. Of course, when you write such a letter, retain a copy. It is good to send a letter confirming insurance coverage by certified mail.

In addition to binding the company, if an agent slips up and fails to cover you for a given loss, either totally or partially, you also probably have a right to proceed against the agent. Most agents carry "errors and omissions" coverage to protect them from mistakes made in their own offices. Once again, the larger and more reputable insurance agencies are more likely to be adequately covered with errors and omissions coverage than the small, solo operators. You may be doing your neighbor a favor by letting his idiot son, right out of high school, write some insurance for you, but you are probably exposing yourself to the risk of losing a potentially "deep pocket" in the event of a mistake! The authors recommend dealing with reputable insurance agencies, capable of writing policies with multiple insurers so that you can get comparative rates, skilled in handling the type of insurance you request.

MAKING CLAIMS—WHAT TO DO WHEN LIGHTNING STRIKES

Having purchased adequate insurance coverage, you need not worry if you sustain a loss, right? All you have to do is call up your friendly agent and he'll see to it that you get paid in full, right? You can comfortably trust your insurance people when it comes to promptly and carefully processing your claim, right? The foregoing assumptions, if made, are probably the most dangerous you could ever make! An analysis of the insurance business quickly tells us why it is wrong to assume that you'll be met with prompt, considerate service when you assert a claim. First, in any organization, there is always a pulling and tugging match between the sales force and the administrative force, particularly when it comes to those who control the fiscal end of the business. Consequently, it is not surprising that the sales end of an insurance business, which consists primarily of its agents, will present an extremely friendly picture when you are in the process of obtaining insurance. On the other hand, the claims department, which is answerable to the controller, does not get gold stars on its chart by throwing away money! In many, if not most insurance companies, the claims department not only handles claims by third parties against its policyholders, it also handles the policyholders' claims. Lumping all claims together at the end of the year, it matters little to the department whether a claims agent has denied a policyholder's claim or that of a third party. When it comes to the bottom line—the percentage of claims, and the dollar amount, paid out—loyalty to policyholders doesn't count for much.

What does this mean to the small businessman? Your authors suggest that if you have a claim, it means being careful from the start. The first document normally submitted to an insurance company after a loss is the proof of loss statement. This is usually preceded by a telephone call to the agent to get the form. Both of these communications are vital. In cases of large losses, your authors recommend consulting with your attorney before either speaking to your agent or submitting a proof of loss statement.

On your own, you should also immediately set out to preserve the evidence of the loss in the form of documentation, photographs, and physical evidence such as broken parts. The same consideration involved in preserving evidence for contractual disputes apply here. Remember, there is a distinct possibility that you will be involved in a lawsuit against the insurance company if they do not fully honor your claim.

There are refreshing exceptions. Generally, however, regardless of how friendly they appear, claims agents are not your friends. What they say to you, what actions they take, and what correspondence they send may also be evidence. After you have had conversations with a claims agent and he has made statements favorable to your claim, make memoranda of them. When he has refused payment or made payment in part, make photocopies of the checks, etc. Retain all correspondence and other documentary evidence. We suggest opening a separate file for each insurance loss claim you make.

When speaking with claims agents regarding large claims, it is a good idea to have conversations witnessed, if at all possible. One way a businessman can do this is to appoint a subordinate employee to work with him in dealing with the claims agent. Having once done so, it is not awkward for the two of you to be present when conversing with a claims agent. Thus, if you find yourself in court at a later date, one of you can corroborate the statements made by the other as well as the statements the claims agent makes to you. If you deal telephonically with the claims agent, the same goal can be accomplished by using a speakerphone in your office. As soon as the important conversation is terminated, the two of you should collaborate in preparing a memorandum of what was said. Do not prepare two memorandums. Inconsistencies may cause problems if the matter has to go to court.

In cases of large losses, insure that you are indeed claiming *all* of your losses. This may require a careful study of your policy by a professional. You may have a claim for business interruption, or other compensable loss, which you have not considered. This, in turn, may give rise to an additional claim for consequential damages to your business, which may require the services of an economist or other expert. The important thing to remember here is not to go running off at the mouth with a claims agent while you are in the process of analyzing what your real loss is. A statement made to him at this time may overlook important areas of loss. It is important to report your losses promptly, in accordance with the terms of your policy. However, in reporting them, it is also important to not commit yourself to any statement which indicates, at a premature time, that you are reporting the totality of your loss.

If you must submit a proof of claim form at an early date, it is a good idea to carefully consider the language used on the form. If you are in doubt, consult with your lawyer. You may well find yourself using such phrases as "complete losses not yet fully ascertained" or "loss evaluation still in process." Such phrases will undoubtedly pique the curiosity of the claims agent, who has a desire to wrap up your claim as quickly as possible. The name of the game here is caution. Do not commit yourself to a bottom line figure until you have completely satisfied yourself that you have spelled out each and every item of loss that your business has suffered. In cases of large and complex losses, this may not be accomplished until you have brought in a lawyer and experts in several fields. Throughout the entire process, your relationship with your insurance company may be friendly, but it has the potential of becoming unfriendly at any moment. The World War II phrase "loose lips sink ships" might be applicable to your business. You should control the number of personnel who deal with the claims agent. If the claims agent wishes to interview various employees, you or the subordinate assigned to the loss should be present. Again, memoranda should be made of what the claims agent heard, said, and saw.

WHAT TO DO IF YOU GET SUED FOR MORE THAN YOUR POLICY LIMITS

Once a matter has been put in suit and the insurance company has agreed to defend me and has provided an attorney, they can be counted upon to look after all of my interests, right? Not necessarily. Whenever a suit is brought for greater than the policy limits, the insurance company is in a situation in which there may be a departure of their interests from yours. The way this can happen is as follows: after a suit has been brought and negotiations commenced, the party who is suing may make a demand that is high, but within the policy limits. For example, assume that you have $500,000 coverage for personal injuries caused by drivers of the vehicles owned by your business. Assume that you have been sued for $1 million as a result of a serious accident caused by the driver of one of your trucks. Assume that a lawsuit has been commenced, discovery has taken place, and the parties are now negotiating settlement. The lawyer for the injured party makes a demand of $490,000 to settle the case, knowing that your policy limits are $500,000. Unless you are consulted and have an opportunity to become involved in the decision-making process, the insurance company probably will flatly reject the demand on the grounds that it is too high. This could force the case to go to trial with the prospect of a possible jury verdict in excess of the policy limits. Unless you are fully advised of all negotiations, the case could go to trial, a verdict could be rendered for greater than the policy limits, and you could be stuck for anything in excess of the $500,000.

In such a case, do you have any recourse? Indeed you do, and indeed, insurance companies frequently do not apprise you of what recourse you have! What can you do in such a case? First, you have a right to insist that you be made aware of all settlement demands in any lawsuit in which you are a personal defendant, particularly when you have been sued for over your limits. Having this right, and being fully informed, you should set out to elicit a demand within the policy limits. Once you have elicited such a demand, you should write your insurance company a letter, directing them to pay the demand. The insurance company is not obligated to make such payments, but if it refuses to do so it is obligated to pay any verdict in excess of the coverage, since such a verdict would be a result of having run the risk of trying the lawsuit contrary to your instructions to settle it in accordance with a demand within your limits. Sometimes, in order to elicit such a demand, you will have to hire a lawyer of your own who will deal directly with the claimant or his lawyer. Once this has been accomplished, you have effectively increased your coverage, as a matter of law, to whatever the verdict calls for. As you are probably aware, however, there are available umbrella coverages which apply in cases where you may be sued for amounts in excess of ordinary liability coverages. However, these umbrella coverages are not always available, and consequently, you may find yourself faced with a suit calling for damages in excess of your coverage.

One note of caution here: the whole business of demands and lawsuits, insurance coverages, etc., can be rather tricky. The authors recommend that you consult an attorney in any case in which you are sued for more than your policy limits.

15

Conclusion

As stated in the introduction, your authors have taken a number of the most common problem areas for the beleaguered businessman and have attempted to give you their best advice as to how to solve them. A great amount of theory and explanation has not been included. There are ample sources available to the businessman if he wishes to educate himself further in business theory, legal theory, and how they relate. We felt it better to leave these matters to others and concentrate on making our advice in this book as succinct as possible. If you are in doubt about any of the advice given in this book, we cannot overemphasize the advisability of consulting with a good business lawyer. He should be willing to give you ample reasons for his advice and also to advise you on the application of anything you find in this book. We hope what we have attempted to convey is useful to you. If you have any ideas on how we can improve this book, or comments upon it, please do not be shy about contacting us. We hope we can improve this book as the years go by, and any input we can obtain from our readers would be most appreciated.

Jerome S. Rice
Keith A. Libbey
Fredrikson, Byron, Colborn,
  Bisbee & Hansen, P.A.
4744 IDS Center
Minneapolis, MN 55402

Glossary

Arm's length. A transaction not involving related parties.

Bankruptcy. A court proceeding to reorganize or liquidate an insolvent person or corporation.

Boiler plate. Common language in an agreement. Also called the "fine print."

Book value. The book value of a company is calculated by subtracting all of its liabilities from all of its assets. The resulting value is the book value.

Chattel paper. The documentation, such as a mortgage deed, that evidences a security interest.

Collateral. Property given to secure a loan.

Co-maker. A co-maker is a surety.

Consequential damages. Such damage, loss, or injury as does not flow directly and immediately from the act of the party but only from some of the consequences or results of that act.

Default. Failure to perform conditions required by an agreement, in this case a loan agreement, such as failure to pay interest or principal when due.

Demand loan. A loan for no fixed period of time due upon demand by the lender.

Endorser. A person who signs an instrument other than a maker for the purpose of transferring, guaranteeing, or acting as a surety on the instrument. An endorsement of payment guaranteed renders one primarily liable whereas an endorsement of collection guaranteed renders one secondarily liable—only after remedies have been exhausted against the primary party. One can also be an endorser on a limited basis not involving a guarantee or surety as when one transfers by endorsement of a check or a note.

Execution. Sometimes more correctly called "writ of execution." An execution is a command to the sheriff, in writing, to levy upon the assets of a judgment debtor.

Exposure. The difference between a loan and the collateral whereby the lender is exposed to loss.

Foreclosure. Action by a lender to take possession of and sell the collateral.

Guarantee language. Words which can be construed to mean a promise to pay somebody else's debt.

Guarantee of collection. A contract whereby the guarantor is liable only after the primary party has been pursued to the exhaustion of the creditor's remedies.

Guarantor. A guarantor is liable on the debt of another person under a separate contract pursuant to an independent undertaking and is secondarily liable only after the primary party defaults on the original obligation and the guarantor is notified thereof.

In terrorem clause. A clause in a contract designed to keep the other party from doing something by terrorizing in an unreasonable fashion. Hence, in most instances, *in terrorem* clauses are unenforceable in court, whereas a liquidated damages clause, which reasonably approximates the actual damages which might be occasioned by a breach of the contract, will be enforced.

Leverage. Increasing the effective use of your assets by borrowing against them.

Levy. The act whereby a sheriff seeks to satisfy a judgment.

Lien. As a noun, a security interest in real estate or property generally occasioned by having improved its value, such as a mechanic's lien on a piece of real estate. A mechanic's lien can be obtained by workmen who have improved the real estate and can be foreclosed to satisfy the debt owed the workmen. As a verb, the act of placing a lien against property.

the real estate and can be foreclosed to satisfy the debt owed the workmen. As a verb, the act of placing a lien against property.

Line of credit. An understanding between a lender and a borrower that the borrower will be entitled to borrow a certain amount for a period of time.

Liquidate collateral. Similar to foreclosure. The conversion of collateral to cash by sale.

Liquidated damages. Damages, the sum of which is determined, by contract, in advance, rather than having to be proved.

Market share. That percentage of the market which the company has obtained by sales of its products.

Preference. The delivery to one creditor of property or collateral by way of transfer in a manner that gives him a greater percentage of recovery on his debt than other creditors generally receive, at a time when the debtor is insolvent and within either 90 days or one year prior to bankruptcy.

Primary party. A person who is liable in the first instance to the creditor and against whom the creditor must first exhaust all his remedies before proceeding against any secondary party.

Prime rate. The rate at which banks will lend money to their most favored customers.

Priority (in bankruptcy). A bankruptcy classification which allows certain debts to be satisfied before others, such as secured creditors coming before unsecured creditors, and so on.

Put. A right to require someone else to purchase your stock.

Quality. A reference to how good or bad a loan might be.

Refinancing. Obtaining a new loan to pay off an old one.

Represent. To make a statement of fact claimed to be true.

Secondary party. A party who has contracted for liability but only after remedies against the primary party have been exhausted. If the secondary party must pay the debt he has a claim against the primary party for the full amount.

Secured lender. One who has made a loan and received collateral to protect the loan.

Security interest. A property right securing a debt, such as a real estate mortgage which secures money advanced by a bank or other lender.

Surety. A surety is bound by the same contract as the principal and is liable as a primary party on the obligation itself.

Term loan. A loan for a fixed period of time.

Usurious. A loan bearing a rate of interest which is higher than the rate permitted by law.

Writ. A judicial order. Some special writs, such as writs of prohibition and writs of mandamus, are issued by supreme courts against lower courts. Writs of prohibition prohibit judges from taking certain actions likely to interfere with a party's rights. Writs of mandamus compel public officials to do certain things. There are other writs such as writs of execution, commanding sheriffs to levy upon the property of judgment debtors.

Index

and buyer's right to sue for
damages, 64–65
and notification of
defectiveness, 65
preservation of evidence of,
65–66
refusal of acceptance of, 64
and remedies of buyer, 59–66
return for repair clauses
covering, 66
revocation of acceptance of,
64
and seller's right to cure, 64

F

Federal Trade Commission, 84
Finance companies, 3
Foreclosure procedures,
restrictions upon, 2
Fraudulent transfers, 31–32

G

Garnishment, definition of, 24

H

*How to Handle Your Own
Lawsuit,* 25

I

Insurance agents
dealing with, 114–115
oral contracts with, 114–115
selection of, 115
Insurance claims
and documenting losses, 116–117

and prompt reporting of all
losses, 117–118
and seeking legal advice
before making large
claims, 116
and submitting a proof of
loss statement, 116
Insurance companies, types of,
113
Insurance contracts
documentary confirmation of,
115
oral, 114–115
Insurance coverage
amount of, 112
with multiple insurers, 113
and perils insured against,
113
suits in excess of, 118–120
yearly review of, 113

L

Law firms, full service,
advantages of, 100
Lawyers
and clients, relations
between, 108–109
contingent fees of, 107–108
and estimates of probable
costs, 105
hourly fees, of, 101–102
reasonable value billing by,
106–107
retainers of, 102–103
and withdrawal for non-
payment of fees, 101–102
Liens, 27–28